THE COMPLETE GUIDE TO
SALTWATER
FISHING

THE COMPLETE GUIDE TO
SALTWATER
FISHING

HOW TO CATCH STRIPED BASS, SHARKS, TUNA, SALMON, LING COD, AND MORE

Al Ristori
Foreword by Angelo Peluso

SKYHORSE PUBLISHING

Skyhorse Publishing books may be purchased in bulk at special discounts for
sales promotion, corporate gifts, fund-raising, or educational purposes. Special
editions can also be created to specifications. For details, contact the Special Sales
Department, Skyhorse Publishing, 307 West 36th Street, 11th Floor, New York, NY
10018 or info@skyhorsepublishing.com.

Skyhorse® and Skyhorse Publishing® are registered trademarks of Skyhorse
Publishing, Inc.®, a Delaware corporation.

Visit our website at www.skyhorsepublishing.com.

10 9 8 7 6 5 4 3 2 1

Library of Congress Cataloging-in-Publication Data is available on file.

ISBN: 978-1-51075-247-4
eISBN: 978-1-51075-248-1

Cover design by Daniel Brount
Cover image courtesy of Al Ristori

Printed in China

To my wife Kathy and children Sherilynn,
Michael and Cyndi who have endured my many absences in the course
of trying to outwit creatures with brains the size of a pea.

Table of Contents

Foreword

Al Ristori is a bonafide superstar within the recreational fishing community. He sits atop a pyramid of worldwide anglers recognized not only for their sport fishing accomplishments but also for their vast contributions to the sport. Al is a master angler, avid sportsman, and dedicated fisheries conservationist who is most willing to share the secrets of his impressive success. From his beginning days on Long Island catching sunfish from a local pond to the vast offshore haunts of the world's oceans, Ristori has amassed a resume filled with diverse and grand saltwater fish species. A 1022-pound grander bluefin tuna, a 409-pound record mako shark, and a 61-pound striped bass are examples of his aptitude for catching remarkable trophy specimens. Al has also held IGFA world records for leather bass, mullet snapper, sea raven, round whitefish and pinfish.

As a former charter boat captain, Ristori's prowess and consistency for catching numerous and large striped bass remain both legendary and unsurpassed. His high level of proficiency at both boat and shore fishing gives Al a unique platform from which to share a wealth of experiences and knowledge. Ristori's accumulated angling wisdom is priceless and an invaluable asset to those who might learn from his achievements. The *Complete Guide to Saltwater Fishing* is the perfect vehicle for communicating to anglers of all levels the pure essence of saltwater fishing; the how, where, when, and why of angling in the brine this comprehensive volume is literally packed cover to cover with critical and to-the-point information that will enhance any angler's success on the water. Whether one fishes from a boat or from the shore, the contents of this book will up your game and add to your basket of fishing skills.

The *Complete Guide to Saltwater Fishing* takes the reader on a skillfully crafted journey of discovery. Methods, techniques, and tactics are explained in a straightforward manner that offers insights into the art of saltwater fishing. The content of this book will benefit novice and expert alike. The fundamentals of the game, such as gear selection, terminal tackle, knots, and profiles of the quarry are presented with clarity and a unique perspective that only a world-class angler like Ristori can proffer. As any devotee of saltwater fishing can attest, there is much more to the angling endeavor than merely casting and retrieving a bait, and two chapters of this book particularly

THE COMPLETE GUIDE TO SALTWATER FISHING

underscore that reality. The chapter on "Understanding the Marine Environment" and the segment on "Techniques" are alone worth the price of admission. Ristori's extensive experience presents a distinctive viewpoint in these chapters that is sure to spark reader interest to embrace his concepts and his assessment of effective methods and techniques. There is no doubt that what is delivered in this book, will enhance the reader's effectiveness and catch consistency on the water.

On a personal note, I have admired for many decades Al's devotion to sport-fishing and his commitment to conservation and protection of various fisheries. He has been at the forefront of those issues well before they became trendy topics. Much of my own growth and development within the world of sportfishing was guided by Al's spoken and written words. I encourage all who enjoy saltwater fishing to read this guidebook and retain it as a handy reference. It will indeed make you a much better angler.

Angelo Peluso
Long Island Sound
October 2019

Introduction

Welcome to the wonderful world of saltwater fishing! When I started riding a bicycle to fish with a canepole in Camman's Pond in Merrick, Long Island, more than a half-century ago, even the stunted sunfish were fascinating. The day I walked across the spit of land between the pond and a saltwater canal and encountered the much bigger and stronger eels, white perch, and snapper bluefish, however, was the day I became a saltwater convert.

That was just the beginning of a lifetime fascination with the wonders of oceans, bays, and tidal rivers—and that fascination has inspired trips around much of the globe to sample saltwater sport and the hundreds of species (some never identified) that swim in those waters. In order to devote a maximum of time to that pursuit and have a reasonable excuse for doing so, I turned my back on anything resembling real work and have made a living in the fishing tackle business and then as a full-time outdoor writer, photographer, and charter captain.

Other fishermen often ask if after all these years I ever tire of fishing, and my reply is always "Of course not." The endless variety of saltwater fishing is a major factor, and I never tire of the challenge involved in pitting my intellect (which includes a Phi Beta Kappa key) against brains the size of peas and often coming up a loser. Anyone who tells you they always fool fish is someone not to be believed!

To be sure, I do fish in fresh waters on occasion, but I can't get excited about seeking dumb stocked fish and have found that saltwater fish are almost invariably stronger, faster, and more spectacular fighters than their freshwater counterparts. That became particularly obvious to me some years ago when I joined a bunch of freshwater writers aboard a large charterboat for a trip, sponsored by Berkely, to the Dry Tortugas at the western end of the Florida Keys. Before making that run, the skipper anchored on a shallow Gulf of Mexico wreck where I started throwing tube lures for barracuda. The midwestern writers were fascinated by the explosions on those tubes by fish which resembled their northern pike, but were amazed when hooked cuda tore off 50 yards of mono while a similar-size pike would be unlikely to take even a turn or two from a similar drag.

That's pretty typical of what those of us with many years fishing in salt waters have come to expect. There's a world of opportunity in those waters, and the information in this book should help lead you to a level of success which, I hope, will make you every bit as enthusiastic as I am about this great sport.

This book has been written with everyone from the beginner to the expert in mind. To accomplish that, there's quite a bit of basic information which old salts will undoubtedly skip through. However, there's enough "meat" beyond those basics to please even those with considerable experience on the ocean. Everything from tackle and techniques to the major species sought in North American waters are covered in upcoming chapters.   —*Al Ristori*

CHAPTER 1
Rods & Reels

There is little in rods and reels except big-game gear which can be exclusively labeled "fresh" or "salt" water tackle. Saltwater anglers use everything from ultralight up, and freshwater fishermen in certain circumstances turn to saltwater outfits such as surfcasting rigs when fishing dams for large striped bass and catfish. All modern rods and reels (except most closed-face reels, which retain moisture and aren't manufactured to handle salt corrosion) are made to take the abuse of salt water and will stand up if anglers remember to rinse them with fresh water after each outing. A good spray of WD-40 or something similar is also beneficial.

As a youngster fishing with cane and beryllium rods, I could hardly imagine the wondrous materials we now take for granted. The introduction of fiberglass after WWII was a quantum leap, and that material has been continually refined ever since. Meanwhile, even more sophisticated materials such as graphite have been developed and are constantly being refined to produce ever tougher, lighter, and more sensitive rods. Every material has good and bad points, and combinations of materials often work out best. For instance, modern E-glass is still the best material for making the toughest of all rods—heavy-duty stand-up models used for tuna. One-piece rods are favored for most purposes by saltwater anglers, but travel considerations often require two-piece construction—especially for long surfcasting models. Spinning rods feature a large gathering guide followed by gradually smaller guides that reduce friction by funneling line to the tip top.

It isn't the quality of the tackle that always matters as young Mike Ristori found while catching his first fish—a tiny gray snapper off a dock in the Florida Keys, on a Snoopy outfit.

Ultralight spinning makes even average-sized weakfish a challenge.

This chapter breaks down tackle into broad categories for various uses. It's important to note that all capacities are expressed in terms of normal monofilament line. The tightly braided lines that have become popular have such small diameters that an adequate supply of 50-pound could be wound onto a light spinning reel, though there would be no point in doing so since the reel simply isn't designed to provide heavy drags. Utilizing the maximum would likely result in stripped gears and broken rods. Look for further discussion of this factor in the Line Chapter.

Balanced tackle is essential for good casting. Manufacturers place line class and lure range recommendations on their rods, and spinning reels usually have approximate capacities for suitable line tests printed on the spool. Modern guides are a huge improvement over what we used only a few decades ago, and most will last longer than their owners.

ULTRALIGHT SPINNING Though primarily thought of as tackle more suited to freshwater streams and ponds, there are many uses for ultralight in salt water. The primary objective is obtaining the maximum enjoyment from relatively small fish that would be easily overpowered on stouter gear, though there are times when the use of ultralight outfits will result in improved catches. Ultralight involves the use of tiny reels holding no more than 100 yards of 6-pound mono mounted on very light one-handed rods of five to five and a half feet. Anglers normally use 2- or 4-pound mono with such outfits, which are fine for school striped bass, bluefish, weakfish, spotted sea trout, some bottomfish, and other species that can be caught in relatively open waters.

Kids like Cyndi Ristori and Kevin Correll can have fun in shallow river waters with ultralight spinning.

Obviously, you're not likely to turn a striper heading for rocks with ultralight tackle, and almost any gamefish will be hard to catch from an anchored boat in a strong current. It may be necessary to chase a fish weighing only a few pounds if it has the current behind it, and that just isn't practical in a situation where other anglers are trying to enjoy themselves. Open-water bottomfish such as flounder are ideal on ultralight in shallow waters, as the feel for bites can't be beat and even relatively lightweight fighters become good sport on that gear. Ultralight is also effective in catching live bait such as pinfish, pilchards, cigar minnows, and small blue runners, though you may have so

Light spinning tackle is perfect for casting jigs to redfish at Captiva Island, Florida.

much fun in the process that you'll forget about going for the larger fish altogether!

LIGHT SPINNING Of far more use in saltwater are the six-and-one-half- to seven-foot spinning rigs with standard-size spinning reels, holding from 200 yards of 6-pound to about 150 yards of 12-pound. The Mitchell 300, imported by Garcia from France, revolutionized this segment of the market during the 1950s and 1960s as the low cost of quality spinning reels put them in even the casual angler's hands. Many advances have been made since then, especially in terms of higher gear ratios, line rollers, more dependable bails, lightness, stainless-steel ball bearings, and saltwater durability. Though the basic rod type dominates the freshwater market for everything from panfishing to trout, bass, and pike, those rods usually have short butts intended for one-handed casting.

Comparable saltwater versions normally have longer butts for two-handed casting, which provides greater distance and more accuracy. The longer butt also helps in fighting tough fish, as it can be braced against your midsection rather than putting all the strain on a wrist. As a general rule, light saltwater rods employ heavier actions than comparable length freshwater models in order to handle heavier lures and apply greater pressure to large fish. Rather than one-quarter-ounce spinners, saltwater anglers are more likely to be using one-half- to three-quarter-ounce plugs and jigs with such outfits. One-piece models are most popular, and it's becoming difficult to find suitable saltwater rods in this class that are two-piece for traveling.

Light spinning outfits cover a wide range of saltwater purposes, including casting in bays and rivers for small gamefish, light bottom fishing, and some use in the ocean when conditions permit using light tackle for larger gamesters. They're perfect for wading tropical flats in search of such species as bonefish and barracuda, and are

Light spinning is the usual choice for flats fishing in the Florida Keys, as John Havlicek, Boston Celtics Hall of Famer, is doing during the annual Islamorada Redbone All-Release Celebrity Tournament.

surprisingly common in the New Jersey surf where anglers typically cast one-half- to one-ounce plugs and jigs for school stripers and bluefish. The occasional much larger striper can often be beached with time and patience.

MEDIUM SPINNING The next step up is in spinning reels with capacities from about 300 yards of 12-pound up to 200 yards of 20-pound, matched to seven- to nine-foot rods to form ideal combinations for casting lures in the surf and from boats. The stiffer seven-footers are also good for a variety of other boat applications, including the use of live or dead bait. Bottom fishing is also possible, though spinning tackle is at a disadvantage here because such reels provide minimal power, thus making the angler work harder in order to move a large fish. On the other hand, the high gear ratios that reduce power are a great advantage in working popping plugs for all species that will attack them, and also for metal lures intended for such species as wahoo and king mackerel, which won't hit slow-moving lures. Some South Florida skippers found years ago that modern saltwater spinning tackle is ideal for slow-trolling live baits such as balao and pilchards for sailfish, king mackerel, blackfin tuna, and many other species that require a short dropback. They use pieces of copper rigging wire to hold the line with the bail open. Shimano then perfected a spinning reel that features a Baitrunner lever that allows baits to be slow-trolled from a closed bail with just enough pressure to keep line from going out. When a strike occurs, a flip of the lever or a turn of the handle will activate the preset drag. Several other companies have adopted that basic system.

Medium spinning works well in most surf conditions for striped bass, such as this one landed by the author at Island Beach State Park, New Jersey.

HEAVY SPINNING The largest spinning reels are quite heavy and not really intended for casting all day. They carry from about 250 yards of 20-pound up to 300 yards or more of 30-pound. These can be used in conjunction with surfcasting rods of nine to 12 feet or more to cast baits well off the beach. Such heavy rigs are particularly important when utilizing heavy sinkers and large baits. Though coastal anglers often purchase long one-piece

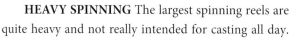

4

surf rods, most are custom-made by tackle shops. Manufacturers serve the mass market with two-piece models that are easier to ship and transport. Be sure to check manufacturer's ratings before buying a model for a particular fishery. For instance, those rated for one to four ounces are fine for casting lures and light baits such as clams and worms, but you'll want heavier models when six- to eight-ounce sinkers are required and baits such as bunker (menhaden) heads are being cast.

Heavy spinning tackle is required when casting poppers for cubera snappers in the tropics.

Large-capacity spinning reels are often used with shorter (six-and-one-half to seven-foot) heavy-duty boat spinning rods for big-game fishing or casting lures to species such as wahoo, which will run off hundreds of yards during their first burst.

BAITCASTING Small conventional reels designed for casting blazed a path in fishing well over a century ago. The modern versions, usually referred to as baitcasters, feature finely-tuned models with levelwind mechanisms that correctly place line on the spool for the next cast. These reels have long been popular for freshwater bass and pike fishing, but are also used extensively in salt water for everything from light bottom fishing up to casting for 100-pound tarpon. Since they provide the power of a conventional reel while still being easy to cast and a pleasure to handle, baitcasters serve well in many saltwater situations, such as chumming and chunking for striped bass and bluefish as well as in strictly casting situations. They're particularly popular on the Gulf of Mexico coast with anglers casting for redfish (red drum) and spotted sea trout.

Though models produced by such firms as Pflueger, Shakespeare, and Coxe were popular before World War II, the arrival of Ambassadeur baitcasters from Sweden in the 1950s created a new standard. Those reels remain among the finest made today, though they've since had strong challenges from manufacturers such as Penn, Daiwa, and Shimano. While some baitcasters intended for strictly freshwater use have smaller capacities, the light

Baitcasting is a good choice when working heavier jigs in deeper water for large weakfish.

5

Light conventional tackle is the norm for catching bottomfish such as these tautog hooked by ex-heavyweight champ Larry Holmes along with Capt. Tommy Joseph and the author out of Shark River, New Jersey.

Medium conventional gear, especially lever-drag models, works well for powerful amberjack in deep waters, as Walt Jennings demonstates off the Florida Keys.

Even medium conventional tackle is light when matched against a 150-pound shark, as ex-Green Bay Packers lineman Jerry Kramer discovered during a long battle off Walker's Cay, Bahamas, before the author placed the tag.

models we use in saltwater take from 200 yards of 12-pound up to 150 yards of 20-pound. Thus, in the Ambassadeur line, saltwater anglers normally opt for the wider-spool 6000 series models rather than the 5000s that are so popular in freshwater. Rods are usually in the six to seven-foot range except for five-and-one-half to six-foot "muskie" rods, and the seven-and-one-half-foot popping rods that are particularly popular with southern anglers seeking spotted sea trout. The stiff muskie rod serves many saltwater purposes, and is easy to travel with, even though it's one piece. I carried a Lamiglas model over much of the globe before it finally got broken in a rod case.

Larger baitcasting reels that still retain the level wind are a better bet when bottom bouncing for fish that have to be immediately moved from their lairs, and for casting, chumming, and trolling for bigger fish that will test the capacity of ordinary baitcasters. When most of the line disappears from the spool, the angler is at a great disadvantage since so much effort has to be expended in getting every inch back onto the spool. The Ambassadeur 7000 has proven to be an ideal size for a great variety of saltwater fishing, as has the Zebco Quantum Iron IR430CX with its 6-1 gear ratio.

CONVENTIONAL TACKLE This is probably the most common tackle associated with saltwater fishing. Many sportfishermen were still using handlines or knuckle-busting sidewinders when Otto Henze started producing Penn reels during

Stand-up big-game tackle enables outstanding anglers such as Dr. David Gong of San Francisco to overpower large yellowfin tuna, such as this one hooked from the author's boat off Montauk, Long Island.

the 1930s, but those reels were so affordable that virtually every saltwater angler soon owned one or more. The basic star-drag models for bottomfish and light trolling are still produced with such efficiency that Asiatic competition has failed to make a dent in Penn's dominance of the market. Bottom fishermen usually match such reels to five-and-one-half to seven-foot rods with medium to heavy actions, depending on the type of fishing—particularly in terms of sinker weight for bottom-fishing.

Penn Senator reels put the average angler into heavy-duty fishing situations ranging all the way up to giant bluefin tuna, even though there were more sophisticated and expensive lever-drag reels available. My largest giant tuna, a 1022-pounder, was caught on a 14/0 Senator. The star drags on those reels require frequent doses of water to dissipate the heat created by big gamefish making long runs, but other than that problem they're quite adequate for the task.

Fin-Nor and several smaller companies produced lever-drag big-game reels for many years prior to Penn's introduction of its International series. Shimano has also become a big factor in that area. Lever drags are much more efficient in fighting big game, and they spread heat over a wide area in order to prevent seizure. The angler is able to select free spool, strike and fighting settings that can be moved in an instant. Though originally only used on heavier reels, lever drags are now available in light trolling and chumming models such as the Shimano TLD and Penn GLS lines.

Big-game rods were traditionally designed for fighting out of chairs. Most were

Fly angler battles a striped bass off Island Beach State Park, New Jersey, during a fall blitz as birds locate the feeding fish.

six-and-one-half to seven-footers with parabolic actions and roller guides. They were fine when used in that fashion, but fighting fish with them from a standing position was torture on the back. West Coast long-range fishermen designed a much better mouse trap with stand-up rods that were only five-and-one-half to six feet with a relatively long foregrip plus a light tip that brings the bend almost back to the angler's hands. That system creates a huge mechanical advantage in favor of the angler, who can now stand up comfortably, with the aid of modern rod belts and kidney harnesses, to fight tuna weighing hundreds of pounds.

7

Giant tuna require the heavy drags produced by the largest lever-drag reels and the added pressure anglers can apply with their legs from a fighting chair.

Though roller guides are still the first choice for big-game guides, modern standard guides of silicon carbide and other such materials have proven to be quite effective in standing up to all types of lines while maintaining a smooth surface and avoiding grooving.

Another specialized form of saltwater tackle involves wire-line trolling. Though a wide variety of conventional reels with metal spools are suitable for wire line, rods must have special guides in order to avoid being quickly grooved. Tungston carbide was the traditional choice, but that material has become difficult to obtain and very expensive as Perfection Tip Co. has become the only manufacturer of carbide guides in the United States. Silicon carbide guides also stand up well to wire, and roller guides are fine as long as they're rolling—but anglers using swivels or bulky knots may find they get hung up in such guides.

FLY Though it remains a small portion of the overall picture, flyfishing has been growing by leaps and bounds in salt water. Those watching Saturday morning fishing shows can hardly avoid seeing tarpon and sailfish being caught on the fly. However, the majority of those practicing that sport utilize more standard tackle (such as 8- or 9-weight) for smaller gamefish such as striped bass, bluefish, weakfish, bonefish, red-fish, and spotted sea trout. Fly tackle is very practical in most shallow-water situations, at least when the wind isn't too brutal, and can be utilized in a variety of ways. The use of fly rods in the surf (10 weights are ideal) has been popular from northern New Jersey beaches for some time, and southern anglers regularly catch big fish on flies by teasing such species as amberjack and cobia within range with live baits. By using 500-grain sinking lines or even leadcore, fly fishermen are able to get down in deeper waters and stronger not only to the above-mentioned gamefish but also to such bottom dwellers as flounder, groupers, and snappers.

Joe Blaze demonstrates that fly tackle can be both fun and efficient at catching fall stripers.

CHAPTER 2

Terminal Tackle

LINES Modern anglers take wonderful fishing lines for granted and can't begin to imagine what their grandparents had to work with. When I started fishing during post-World War II days, linen was the standard fishing line. When used in salt water, linen had to be washed off in fresh water and dried in order to prevent rotting. I remember using the posts in our Merrick, Long Island, basement to hold the line from my reel until it was dry and ready to be put back onto the spool. It was a huge advance when I first used monofilament (a World War II invention) on my original spinning reel—a Ny-O-Lite model made of basically the same material—nylon. Not knowing anything about how to place mono on a reel to avoid twist, I ended up with a huge mess that I had to straighten out foot by foot. Once I got used to mono, however, there was no turning back as it was not only less visible in the water but also required no care at all!

MONOFILAMENT The original monos were relatively stiff and not very abrasion-resistant. They've been improved greatly over the years and still are a best bet when very low cost is measured against productivity. Mono is extruded to various diameters, which determines its breaking strength. Depending on the formulation and manufacturing process, mono can be formed to emphasize certain characteristics such as abrasion resistance, but invariably there's a payback in terms of other desirable features such as suppleness. The net result is that mono is a bundle of compromises, though one should be right for the particular form of fishing you pursue. Unfortunately, determining that will involve some experimentation unless you simply want to accept the recommendation of a pro in that fishery. Anglers should be aware that mono is rated well below its breaking strength. This situation started as a reaction to state weights and measures agencies insisting that lines had to test at least as much as stated. Extruding isn't that accurate, so companies started overtesting. Then, as improved technology provided smaller diameters per pound test, they used that advantage to even further overtest and thus make claims such as "the strongest 12-pound" and so on. As a result, most 8-pound lines will test more like 10- or

Yellowfin tuna can be very line shy at times, and fluorocarbon leaders are often the key to success, as the author and his daughter Cyndi demonstrate.

12-pound, which is fine unless such a line is submitted to the International Game Fish Association (IGFA) for a line-class world record. Those seeking such records should use lines with a rating below the class they're fishing in and have them pre-tested. The alternative is to buy IGFA-rated lines from companies such as Ande, which guarantee they'll test in the proper line class. An IGFA 8-pound should test about 7.25- to 7.5-pound breaking strength, which is about 25 percent less than an ordinary 8-pound.

FLUOROCARBONS This formulation has taken over as the only choice for anglers requiring nearly invisible lines for spooky fish. Though expensive when compared to mono, fluorocarbon has a refractive index much closer to that of water. Though you can see it in daylight just as well, it almost disappears in the water and allows anglers to use heavier leaders while still getting strikes. Tuna chunkers have found it to be invaluable when fishing for those sharp-eyed fish in clear waters—particularly during daylight. Some companies have created softer versions of fluorocarbon as fishing line because, unlike mono, it's virtually solid, doesn't absorb water, and sinks—a factor that can help with jigs and diving plugs but may be a problem with light surface lures. Though stiffer than mono, fluorocarbon is more abrasion-resistant and less likely to be damaged by the sun's rays. Some manufacturers are now combining the best qualities of mono lines into what Yo-Zuri appropriately calls Hy-Brid. This brings the cost down while eliminating the water absorption problem of mono.

BRAIDS Back in the 1960s, anglers were delighted to be able to put aside braided nylon lines while switching to mono. Braided nylon cast well enough on conventional reels, but was too soft for spinning and was a poor fishing line since it absorbed water and was very stretchy. Braided Dacron was developed by DuPont and quickly caught on with big-game fishermen because it had very low stretch and stood up indefinitely. However, those casting with conventional reels found it was too "hot" under the thumb, and most turned to mono as softer formulations were developed. A method of braiding that creates a very tight braid was developed in the 1990s; those lines, such as Spiderwire, became popular for both spinning and casting as line test diameter was about a quarter of the comparable mono breaking strength, and there was virtually no stretch. Some anglers soon came to swear by them while others only swore at the tiny, supple line while trying to untangle backlashes and tie one of the few knots that won't slip out. Casting even greater distances is possible with braids, as is the use of lighter, smaller-capacity reels. In experimenting with Berkely FireLine and with Power Pro for surfcasting, I've found that very small diameters are hard to handle while casting into the wind, even if their breaking strength is more than adequate. By going to 50-pound test I still have a small diameter while eliminating constant wind knots, which are very difficult to pick out of braided lines.

Saltwater fly fishermen like Joe Blaze strip with two hands to provide the fast retrieve required for many species.

The very best application for braided lines is in bottom fishing, particularly in deep waters, as every nibble can be sensed and much less sinker weight is required to hold bottom. Unfortunately, braided lines also create an unholy mess when they tangle with mono lines, and I try to stay as far away as possible from other anglers when party boat fishing. Anglers must be cautious with their fingers as the new braideds cut like a knife when line is pulled off against the drag. It's also important to back spools with mono as the entire load of braided line can slip and create the impression of no drag. Knot slippage is another problem, and only certain knots are reliable with these braids. Using a 12-pound-diameter braid that tests about 50 pounds is also a problem in terms of rod breakage. Anglers must be careful when breaking out of the bottom not to wrap the line on their hands. The best bet is to carry a wooden dowel for wrapping the line so the pull can be made on the wooden surface.

FLY LINES Great advances have been made in fly lines over the years, which is a great thing for the sport since the line is the key factor in fly fishing, not the rod and reel. With the right fly line, even a beginner may be able to outfish a pro lacking the proper line. Lines are manufactured to sink at various rates, with some going down so fast that fly fishermen often just flip them out and strip line before working the fly deep, just as a spin fisherman does with a jig. Fly lines are rated from 1 to 15, which ranges from ultralight to big game. Those numbers are based on the amount of grams the flyline weighs in its first 30 feet. Fly rods are designated by the line number they're created for. The specific gravity of the line determines the rate at which it sinks or

Heavy, fast-sinking fly lines enable anglers to plumb the depths when stripers aren't showing and come up with catches such as this striper by Tom Fote off northern New Jersey.

whether it will float. Intermediate lines are the usual choice in salt water, though quick sinkers are a must when you're fishing deeper waters and strong currents. Fly lines also come in various tapers, with weight forward and shooting tapers being most common.

LEAD CORE Braided line with a core made of lead serves to carry lures deeper while trolling. Though somewhat bulky, they can be used on any conventional reels and rods with ordinary guides. Due to the bulk and the braided sheath, lead core isn't very efficient in strong currents and deep water, but it's a good choice in shallow bays and rivers or when trolling close to shore. Back in the 1960s I stumbled onto lead core for trolling Hoochy Trolls in Pleasant Bay on Cape Cod when striped bass were feeding on squid. That proved ideal in the 15-foot depths where surface trolling didn't draw many hits and wire line sunk to bottom too readily, thus requiring more boat speed

Stealth and accurate casting in skinny water is required for bonefish such as this one being fought by Bob Stearns at Sandy Point, Bahamas.

than desired. Lead core is also good for slow trolling live baits such as herring and menhaden. Flyfishermen found lead core enabled them to get flys down into the strike zone while fishing for tarpon in Rio Parismina, Costa Rica, back in the 1970s, but most now use sophisticated fast-sinking fly lines.

WIRE LINE The most difficult line to use is also the most efficient in many saltwater situations. Wire must be used on conventional reels and should be backed with mono or braided line. Monel is the ideal choice due to its flexibility, but stainless steel is half the price and will do the same job of getting lures deep while trolling. Handling of wire line will be discussed in the Techniques chapter.

HOOKS Hooks come in so many sizes and shapes that you'd need a book to explain them all in detail. Certain shapes of standard J-hooks have proven best for various species, but circle hooks are becoming accepted in most cases because hooking is simple and fish can usually be released unharmed. If all the various styles aren't confusing enough, sizing is a mystery to all but dedicated anglers. Rather than simply increasing in size as the numbers get higher, hooks get smaller from number 1 up. For instance, a No. 20 would be a tiny freshwater fly hook. Larger hooks (including the majority used in salt water) then start at 1/0 and go up, with a 12/0 being the size used for giant tuna, large billfish, and sharks. That sizing is based of the width of the hook's gap. As if that's not too confusing, the sizing of circle hooks by many manufactures bears no resemblance to their J hooks. For instance, a Mustad 10/0 circle hook is suitable for school striped bass rather than sharks and tuna—while Eagle Claw circle hook sizes are more comparable to their standard hooks. Hooks also vary in wire strength and diameter, type of point, shank length, eyes, coating, finishes, manufacturing method, and material.

Wire line trolling with Danny plugs at night off Montauk during late fall produced these two 50-pound stripers for the author.

Circle hooks look like they couldn't possibly work, but they're very efficient for fish that turn away after picking up baits. The circle hook is designed to pull out of the fish's stomach or throat and catch in the corner of the jaw. Striking will prevent it from accomplishing that task, so the "secret" to setting circle hooks is simply to bow the rod to the fish and then reel tight. There is a big difference in circle hooks between the standard models and those that are slightly off-centered in order to make baiting them easier. Off-center models work well, but will catch in the stomach if swallowed, whereas the standard circle hook will almost always pull out to catch in the jaw.

TERMINAL GEAR Filling up a tacklebox with the odds and ends required for various types of fishing is no problem at all. Swivels, snaps, fishfinders, wire or mono leaders, split-shot, sinkers, and more pile up because you never know what you might need under particular circumstances. The key is to keep it simple! Use only what is necessary, and then go as light as possible. For instance, when chunking for tuna, a swivel is necessary when free-lining in order to avoid line twist. However, the weight of hook, leader, and swivel carries the bait below the free-floating chunks and makes the presentation less natural. Therefore, the lightest hook, leader, and swivel practical will improve the presentation and fool fussy fish. The same applies with sinkers in a bottom-chunking presentation for striped bass, as a sinker light enough to be lifted and dropped back with the current allows the angler to cover more water and is less obvious to the quarry.

LURES There's an unending variety of lures that can be used in saltwater. Most freshwater lures will work under certain circumstances, but many saltwater lures were developed with specific species or types of fishing in mind. One of the most distinctive is the squid jig, which is used to catch live baits for tuna and other species. Squid are actually classed as shellfish, but they are just as aggressive as finfish. Some can be hooked on ordinary lures and hooks, but the most efficient means of catching them is with nearly weightless lures of various shapes that feature a row of pins around the base which grab the squid when it hits and make it easy to upend them in a bucket quickly before you get blasted with their ink.

Plugs vary infinitely in sizes, shapes, and action. My favorites are popping plugs, as I love nothing more than watching a gamefish hit a surface lure. However, poppers will not do the job at all times, and swimmers are a much more dependable choice at most times for more consistent production. Almost all plugs these days are manufactured from synthetic materials, though a few specialists, such as the successors to Stan Gibbs, still produce wooden plugs that involve so many processes that they're

invariably quite expensive. Plugs can be designed to run at various depths on mono from the surface down to 25 or 30 feet, such as is the case with the Mann's Stretch 25 and 30. Many can only be trolled slowly, while others, such as the Rapala CD series, are made to be trolled at speeds exceeding five knots. Wire line and lead core can be used to carry plugs to specific depths. Uses of specific types of plugs will be detailed in the Techniques chapter.

Leadhead jigs are often referred to collectively as bucktails, though they're

Circle hooks are not only efficient, but by hooking fish in the corner of the mouth they make it possible to release with almost no mortality.

Plugs are a basic for many species, including striped bass, as Tom O'Connor and Jim Beshada discovered while trolling this MirrOlure 113MR off Lavallette, New Jersey.

more commonly used these days with soft plastic bodies or Berkley Gulp for a wide variety of species. The relatively inexpensive bodies are chewed up quickly by sharp-toothed species such as bluefish, and only last for a few large fish with duller teeth. Leadheads come in many sizes, from 1/32-ounce ultralight jigs to eight-ounce or more heads designed for big fish in deep waters. Selecting the right size head for the fishing at hand is critical, as too much weight will drag on the bottom and not look realistic (while also picking up weed, shells, and other debris), while too little won't make it to the pay-off zone. Pork rind is frequently added to bucktails in order to provide a tantalizing tail action. A variation of that jig is the parachute, which utilizes artificial hair wrapped in both directions so it "blossoms" when jigged. Parachutes are standard for wire-line trolling for striped bass and bluefish at Montauk, New York.

Metal jigs come in two basic forms, those designed primarily for casting and retrieving, and those designed for quick sinking and jigging off bottom. These lures can be used for both purposes, but their shape dictates what they're best for. Casting metals come in a variety of sizes from a one-quarter ounce up and are typified by the Hopkins No=Eql, a relatively expensive lure stamped out of stainless steel. Without anything to rust or any coating to chip off, Hopkins will remain fishable in your tack-lebox indefinitely. Both the longer standard model and the rounder Shorty cast very well and have some action, though a jigging motion during retrieve often improves results. Other metal casting lures such as the Luhr Jensen Krocodile and Acme Kast-master feature shapes that produce more action but may not cast quite as well into a wind. All can also be dropped to bottom, but their shapes result in a slower drop that can be good in shallow water but may work against you when trying to reach fish in deep water. Specialized West Coast jigs are utilized for casting to wahoo, a species that requires a very fast retrieve.

Diamond jigs actually come in several forms, but all are designed for a fast drop to bottom, at which point they can be jigged in place or retrieved vertically. Older models, such as the original Bridgeports, had either a treble hook on a split ring or a single hook embedded in the lure. The modern diamond was refined by

A Yo-Zuri Surface Cruiser pencil popper cast by Bud McArthur fooled this bluefin trevally at Isla Montousa, Panama.

Artie Frey during the 1970s and features a single hook on a swivel. Frey's Ava jig hooked just as well, prevented fish from getting a purchase on the jig to twist off, and made removal of the catch in the boat much easier. All sorts of fish-eaters will attack metal jigs, including tunas, but they're especially effective on bottom dwellers. Sizes range from one ounce up to 24 ounces or more, with one-half to one-and-one-half-pound models being used primarily for jigging cod and pollock in deep waters and strong currents off New England. Tube tails are frequently added to diamonds and are a best bet for the toothy bluefish, as they tend to hit farther astern at the tube and stay well away from the mono leader, which provides much better action than wire. Adding a strip of bait to metal or leadhead jigs can often make all the difference when jigging for groupers and snappers in areas where they've been fished hard.

Rollie Schmitten, former chief of the National Marine Fisheries Service, used a metal jig to catch this school striper aboard the author's boat off Manasquan Inlet, New Jersey.

Metal spoons are similar to casting jigs such as the Krocodile. Some spoons are designed for casting in shallow waters and are particularly effective for small red drum (redfish or puppy drum) and Spanish mackerel. Most are intended for trolling either on the surface or weighted down with drails or wire line. Some are very specialized. The bunker spoon, example, is a huge spoon designed to imitate an adult menhaden (bunker, porgy, fat-back),

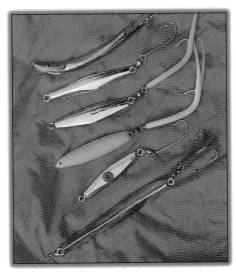

Variety of metal jigs for bottomfishing, with and without tubes. Bottom jig is typical of those used for cod and pollock in deep water.

Lou Grazioso with striper trolled on a
Montauk bunker spoon in Raritan Bay,
New Jersey.

Jethead and Moldcraft high-speed lures
for marlin and tuna.

and was originally fashioned from the reflectors from car headlights. Bunker spoons are used almost exclusively from New Jersey to Rhode Island, where they are run on wire line to tempt large striped bass.

High-speed trolling lures are standards among offshore trollers on all coasts unless those skippers prefer to troll slower with bait. These lures come in many forms, but are all designed to troll at seven knots or more. The head determines whether the lure will run straight or have a somewhat erratic action, and most are intended to pop through the surface at times. Jet heads feature holes in the head to create even more of a bubbling effect. These lures range from about an ounce with a three-inch skirt up to heavier models over a foot long, and will attract everything from little tunny, Spanish mackerel, and skipjacks, up to the largest bigeye tuna and marlins. Though

most high-speed lures have a metal head and a skirt, Mold Craft has long produced an effective line of soft-molded lures for offshore trolling that feel more realistic when mouthed by billfish.

Offshore trollers carry lots of high-speed
lures in various head shapes, lengths,
and colors.

CHAPTER 3

The Species

Fish fall into only three classes. Agnatha, which are rare jawless fish of no angling interest; Chondrichthyes, which are cartilaginous fish such as sharks, skates, and rays; and Osteichthyes, which are the bony fishes that get most of our attention. The scientific breakdown then consists of order, family, subfamily, tribe, genus, and species. Each species has a scientific name that separates it from all others. That name is in Latin so it doesn't vary throughout the world, and consists of two words. The first is shared by the rest of the genus and is always capitalized. The second is specific to the species and can be descriptive or a tribute to a place or individual. The American Fisheries Society has established official common names for every species, and these are listed in this chapter along with the scientific name. In many cases the fish has different names in various areas, and these are also noted. Those local names can cause confusion, especially in the case of the little tunny *(Euthynnus alletteratus),* which is hardly ever referred to by its proper name. Instead, it becomes false albacore or simply "albacore" in the Mid-Atlantic and "bonito" to the south and in the Gulf of Mexico. Those names confuse it with the real albacore found offshore in the Pacific and in canyons off the Mid-Atlantic states, as well as with the real bonito found in Mid-Atlantic waters. Ironically, both albacore and bonito are fine eating fish, while the little tunny, though a great gamefish, is the poorest of the tunas for food.

To allow the reader to easily locate species of interest, the oceanic billfish, tuna, and sharks are covered in a separate section; then comes a section on other tropical and semi-tropical species of the Atlantic and Gulf, plus some in Central America; a third covers the cooler water Atlantic species found primarily above

The little tunny may be the most misidentified of all species, but can easily be identified by the black spots under the pectoral fins.

Cape Hatteras; and the last describes the temperate and cold water fish from California to Alaska. Basic descriptions of the most important species are included, and in cases where they can be easily confused with others the significant differences are noted. Also included is some information about lifestyle, habitat and, most important, how to catch them. The ranges provided typically cover extremes at which the species can only be expected to be found at certain seasons and possibly just during some years when conditions are perfect. The average weights reflect what the angler is likely to catch under normal circumstances. Trophy sizes will normally be much larger, and the International Game Fish Association (IGFA) all-tackle world record for each species as of the 2012 Yearbook is provided as a guide to maximum size. In cases where much larger specimens have been recorded by means other than angling, that is noted as well.

BILLFISH

These are the glamour fish of warm offshore waters, with at least one species being available to anglers in every coastal state except those in the Pacific Northwest. The Billfish Fishery Management Plan of the National Marine Fisheries Service (NMFS) reserves all billfish except swordfish to recreational fishing in the Atlantic and Gulf of Mexico. This fishery has become almost entirely a catch-and-release situation except for some big-money tournaments or the possibility of a record catch. Though the marlins have been overfished, primarily by foreign longliners and as by-catch kill by American longliners who must release them, there is still good fishing in many areas at prime periods. Anglers must be prepared to put in considerable time in order to achieve success, however.

Capt. Ron Mallet about to release a small sailfish off Fort Lauderdale.

ATLANTIC SAILFISH *(Istiophorus platypterus)*
Range: Atlantic Coast, primarily off Florida, but commonly north to Virginia in the summer; Gulf of Mexico, and Caribbean Sea.
Weight: Average 30-50 pounds. Minimum size for retention—63 inches from tip of lower jaw to fork of the tail. While even a 75-pounder is considered very large in U.S. waters, sailfish grow much larger on the other side of the Atlantic. The IGFA world record is 141 pounds 1 ounce, taken off Angola in 1994.

By far the most abundant of Atlantic billfish, this species, unlike others, is generally found close to shore along the Atlantic coast. That's especially the case in southern Florida where the Gulf Stream comes within a few miles of the beach. Sails tend to be found on the inner edge of the Stream, are regularly caught by driftboats fishing for king mackerel in 80 to 150 feet, and have even been hooked from ocean fishing piers. As the Gulf Stream moves offshore farther north, so do the sails. In the Gulf of Mexico it's also necessary to run much farther offshore into blue water. There's no mistaking sailfish for anything else due to their long, sail-like dorsal fin. This fast-growing and very short-lived species tends to congregate in certain feeding areas, and they often work together in order to "ball the bait" (concentrate schools of bait in ever-smaller circles for easy feeding) off Florida's Gold Coast during northerly winter blows. It's at such times that releases of several dozen per boat may be reported as skippers back down on the feeding fish and flip baits to them for one quick release after another. Most sailfish used to be taken by trolling balao or strip baits, but modern Florida sails seem to be much more sophisticated and the use of expensive live baits, particularly goggle-eyes, is almost essential off Palm Beach, while Florida Keys skippers catch most of their sails on live pilchards or balao. Light tackle is a must for this great gamefish, which has been reputed to be the fastest of all fish. Long runs and spectacular jumps on 12- to 20-pound conventional, baitcasting or spinning tackle makes sailfishing among the most popular of saltwater fishing adventures.

PACIFIC SAILFISH *(Istiophorus platypterus)*

Range: Pacific coast from Baja California, Mexico to Peru.

Weight: 100-pounders are average along the Pacific coast from Costa Rica south, while a mixture of sizes farther north includes many 70- to 80-pounders and some

even smaller off Guatemala and southern Mexico. Pacific sails over 140 pounds are uncommon, though some close to 200 pounds have been reported off Ecuador. The long-standing IGFA world record of 221 pounds was caught off Santa Cruz Island in the Galapagos just after World War II in 1947, though there's been nothing close to it since.

Sailfish always put on a great show, as Joe Blaze experiences in the Pacific off Guatemala.

As you'll note by checking out the scientific name, there is no anatomical difference between Atlantic and Pacific sailfish, which have been separated by the IGFA for record purposes because the Pacific version averages twice the size. Though both are spectacular, I don't consider the Pacific sail to be as strong a fighter, pound for pound, as the Atlantic version. Once again, light tackle is suitable, with 20-pound being perfect, and no more than 30-pound being required for even the largest sails. Most run and jump themselves out within 10 minutes. Trolled balao or other small fish are the usual baits in the Pacific, and lures also work well. Some skippers practice the bait and switch technique, in which high-speed lures without hooks are trolled to attract sails, which are then teased toward the boat as a bait is dropped back on appropriate tackle or a fly is cast after the boat is taken out of gear. There is no other big-game fish so easy to fool with a fly, and any properly-equipped angler with even modest casting skills is almost assured of catching a sail during a brief stay at such Pacific sailfishing meccas as Iztapa, Guatemala, and Quepos, Costa Rica during the winter. Daily releases at Guatemala are regularly counted in the dozens, and the use of circle hooks in baits ensures almost 100 percent live releases.

WHITE MARLIN *(Tetrapturus albidus)*

Range: Atlantic coast north to Cape Cod; Gulf of Mexico, and Caribbean Sea.

Weight: Average 40-60 pounds. Though few whites are boated except in tournaments, the official minimum size for retention is 66 inches measured from the tip of the lower jaw to the fork of the tail. Tournaments usually set a minimum of 60 to 65 pounds for weighing. White marlin are generally most abundant during the fall off La Guaira, Venezuela, but the largest have been encountered off Brazil, where the IGFA world record of 181 pounds 14 ounces was taken at Vitoria in 1979.

Whites in the 100-pound class are rarely taken in U.S. waters, especially by the

Kathy Ristori caught this 99 1/2-pound white marlin, which is very large for the species, while sharking off Montauk.

usual method of trolling. Almost all of the few heavyweights taken each year are caught by anglers chumming for sharks, chunking for giant tuna, or chunking at night in the canyons for yellowfin tuna. White marlin can be readily separated from the much larger blue marlin by the rounded, rather than pointed, tips of the pectoral fins and both the first dorsal and first anal fins. Many anglers regard the white as the best fighter among the marlins on a pound-for-pound basis, though they are invariably much smaller. Unfortunately, many are caught on heavy tackle intended for blue marlin or tunas. No more than 30-pound is required when fishing specifically for these marlin, which feature great speed, lots of jumps, and considerable endurance. In the Gulf of Mexico, whites tend to be found well offshore in the Loop Current. They used to be fairly common in relatively inshore areas such as the Jack Spot off Ocean City, Maryland, and Butterfish Hole off Montauk, New York, but very few have been seen in such areas for decades. Except for those found in the nearby Gulf Stream off Hatteras and Oregon Inlet, North Carolina, white marlin fishing has been primarily a far offshore canyon sport in recent years. Relatively few whites are encountered in the Gulf Stream off Florida, but they're much more common on the east side in the Bahamas. Trolling accounts for all whites except the very few caught in chum or chunk lines. Both dead baits such as balao, small mullet, and eels, and high-speed lures work well. If whites can be spotted, small live baits cast to them are almost a sure thing. That sort of fishery may occur during the summer off Martha's Vineyard and Nantucket, Massachusetts.

STRIPED MARLIN *(Tetrapturas audax)*
Range: Eastern Pacific from California south to Peru; also Hawaii.
Weight: Average 90-175 pounds, but up to 500 pounds in the western Pacific. Striped marlin off New Zealand average about twice the size of those in the eastern Pacific. The IGFA world record of 494 pounds was set off Tutukaka, New Zealand, in 1986.

Striped marlin are the most common marlin in the Pacific, and are that ocean's equivalent of the Atlantic's white. Though the fish is twice as large on average, many scientists feel the striped is identical to the white. Striped marlin can't be misidentified due to the blue or lavender stripes on the sides and blue spots on the fins—all of which are still prominent after death. Striped marlin often light up in a fluorescent blue when they're about to strike or when brought alongside. The sides are very compressed as compared to the bulky appearance of blue and black marlin, and the pointed first dorsal fin is higher than on other marlin. Striped marlin are surface fish which are usually spotted and baited, rather than being raised by blind trolling. They may be

Striped marlin such as this one caught off Salinas, Ecuador, are easily identified by their stripes.

caught on dead baits such as balao, mullet, and flying fish, but live baits of a similar size such as mackerels, jacks, and even bottomfish are much more effective. Indeed, at the capitol of striped marlin fishing, Cabo San Lucas at the tip of Baja California, the vast majority of striped marlin caught in recent years have been on live baits cast to them. Unlike the other marlin, striped marlin prefer cooler currents mixing with warm waters, such as those which occur with the Humboldt Current off Salinas, Ecuador. The best fishing for them off Cabo San Lucas occurs in the winter when water temperatures are only in the mid-60s. These fish are great leapers and do almost all their fighting on the surface. Due to greater size and fighting ability than sailfish, 30-pound tackle is recommended, though 20-pound is also reasonable.

BLUE MARLIN *(Makaira nigricans)*

Range: Atlantic north to Cape Cod; Pacific from Mexico south to Peru plus Hawaii.
Weight: Average 200-500 pounds, up to 2000 pounds. Minimum size for retention in the Atlantic—99 inches from the tip of the lower jaw to the fork of the tail.

Pacific and Atlantic blue marlin are the same species, but the IGFA maintains separate record classifications. Blue marlin are almost exclusively taken from deep ocean waters, though they do regularly travel within 20 miles of shore in the Gulf Stream off Hatteras, North Carolina and are caught within sight of shore in many tropical areas including Hawaii, the entire west coast of Central and South America down to Peru, and off Venezuela in the Caribbean. For anglers from Virginia north, the blue marlin is basically a canyon fish, but some of the largest Atlantic blues have been caught in those far offshore waters. Both the New Jersey and New York state records are over 1000 pounds. The largest Atlantic blues have usually come from St. Thomas in the Virgin Islands during the big summer full moon bites, but the current IGFA mark is a 1,402-pound 2-ounce catch from Vitoria, Brazil, in 1992. The Pacific record is slightly smaller at 1,376 pounds off Kona, Hawaii by Jay deBeaubien in 1982. One over 1,800 pounds was caught there on rod and reel, but it failed IGFA recognition because

Blue marlin are a prized catch in many big tournaments, and only the very largest are brought in to contend for prizes in contests such as the Mid-Atlantic $500,000, which has a 400-pound minimum.

24

several fishermen fought it. Blues can be distinguished from whites by the pointed, rather than rounded, dorsal, pectoral, and anal fins as well as the much bulkier body. Pacific blues are separated from the similar black marlin by the fact that their pectoral fins are never rigid and can be folded against the sides even in death. This oceanic wanderer is considered to be one of the finest gamefish as well as a great leaper. Almost all are taken by trolling high-speed lures or dead baits such as mullet, balao, Spanish mackerel, bonefish, and smaller members of the tuna family. Live baiting is very effective when possible, with small tunas and dolphin making ideal baits.

BLACK MARLIN *(Makaira indica)*

Range: Pacific coast from Baja California to Peru plus Hawaii.

Weight: Average 200-500 pounds, up to 2,000 pounds. The IGFA world record of 1,560 pounds is one of the oldest on the books, taken in 1953 by the great big-game fisherman Alfred Glassel Jr. at Cabo Blanco, Peru.

As noted above, blacks are most readily distinguished from the similarly sized blue by the rigid pectoral fins which cannot be folded back against the body without breaking the joints. As with blues, any black over 300 pounds is almost surely a female. Blacks will hit all the same lures and baits as blues but are much more oriented to specific feeding areas such as deepwater reefs and banks like Panama's Hannibal Bank and Pinas Reef, where they prefer slow-trolled live baits such as the various smaller tunas. Blacks tend to fight deeper and may be less spectacular jumpers than blues, particularly as they get older.

Black marlin caught by the author at Hannibal Bank, Panama is about to be clipped free by John Joy. Note rigid pectoral fin.

LONGBILL SPEARFISH *(Tetrapturus pfluegeri)*

Range: Atlantic coast north to Cape Cod; Gulf of Mexico.

Weight: The IGFA world record of 127 pounds 13 ounces was caught in 1999 at the Canary Islands.

Spearfish are the most unusual of billfish, resembling a white marlin with most of its bill cut off. They tend to live farther offshore, are only an occasional catch, and can't be specifically fished for anywhere. Generally, these small billfish are caught on tackle that's far too heavy for them. The longbill has a bill about twice as long as its lower jaw, plus a slender body with a pointed first dorsal fin that looks like a cross between that of a marlin and a sailfish. Though spearfish are short-lived and uncommon, NMFS has prohibited retention in the Atlantic and Gulf of Mexico despite the lack of any information that would indicate they're overfished. The similar shortbill spearfish *(Tetrapturas angustirostris)*, the Pacific version, has a very short bill and pectoral fin. The shortbill is fairly common off Hawaii and may be retained by anglers.

SWORDFISH *(Xiphias gladius)*

Range: Worldwide in temperate and tropical oceanic waters.

Size: Average 40-200 pounds, perhaps up to 2,000 pounds. The IGFA record of 1,182 pounds was caught in 1953 at Iquique, Chile by big-game pioneer Lou Marron, and is one of the oldest on record.

Longlining has devastated swordfish populations throughout the world, with the result that very large swords (over 400 pounds) are now a great rarity. The longline catch now consists primarily of swords under 100 pounds, with numerous sub-legal pups thrown back dead. The last bastion of larger swords in the Atlantic is far at sea on the Grand Banks and Flemish Cap. The glory days of the early 1950s at Iquique have never been repeated, and Marron's all-tackle world record is one of the likeliest to last indefinitely, as are the two women's marks set then—a 772-pounder on 80-pound by Mrs. Lou Marron and a 759-pounder on 130-pound by Mrs. D. A. Allison. Unlike the other billfish, swordfish are considered a commercial species, with the sportfishing catch now so small that it's dismissed as incidental. Swords are also called broadbills, which refers to its very long, wide, smooth, and flattened bill. They also lack ventral fins, and the adults have no scales. This is by far the best-eating of the billfish, a fact which has led to their virtual demise as a sportfish. Most of the commercial catch used to be larger swords harpooned on the surface, where they tend to rest after feeding in the depths and are very easy to approach. Once a common sight off eastern Long Island, where sportsmen trolled dead baits to them and then dropped the baits in hopes that one in 10 would follow it down and get hooked, it's now a rarity to see a sunning sword in

With tag placed, the crew prepares to release the author's swordfish caught off Venezuela.

the Atlantic. Almost all now are taken on lines fished deep in the canyons at night. That fishery still has its moments off southern Florida in the winter and in the northern canyons primarily during September. Daytime swordfishing in even deeper waters was pioneered in recent years by Capt. Richard Stanczyk of Bud N' Mary's Marina in Islamorada, Florida—and has become one of the most consistent means of catching a swordfish. Surfacing swordfish are still reasonably common off southern California, where anglers cast live baits to them. In addition to the odds against one of those dozing swords taking a bait, most of those hooked are lost due to hooks pulling out of the soft mouth. As a result, two-hook rigs are most popular, and even then a high percentage of those boated end up snagged. Large squid is the most popular bait, as that's what swords tend to feed on at night. However, a variety of large fish baits will work. The most consistent sportfishery occurs off La Guaira, Venezuela, which swords can be caught during the day in 250 fathoms and closer to the surface at night. While large squid are imported for those swords, local fishermen also use octopus, Spanish mackerel, little tunny, jacks, and many other small fish for bait. Yet, inspection of one large sword's stomach contents revealed nothing but cutlassfish stacked side-by-side.

TUNAS

When it comes to speed, strength, and durability, the tuna tribe reigns supreme, lacking only the leaping ability of some other great gamefish. According to the IGFA, bluefin tuna have been clocked at speeds up to 43.4 mph in bursts of 10 to 20 seconds. While huge marlin are often caught on very light lines if they fight on the surface and give the crew a shot at them, tuna records on the same lines are only a fraction of the size since they fight deep and rarely provide such suicidal shots. Almost invariably, you'll have to fight your tuna to almost its last gasp. One reason for the exceptional power of the tunas is the fact that they're not completely cold-blooded. Their body temperature can be as much as 18°F higher than the surrounding water. It has been estimated that such a rise in body temperature effectively triples the power and response of a muscle mass. Due to the heat built up in a hooked tuna's body, it's important that it be bled upon capture and kept cool to assure the best eating quality.

BLUEFIN TUNA (*Thunnus thynnus*)
Range: North Atlantic to Gulf of Mexico; temperate Pacific waters from California south.
Weight: Caught in all sizes from 10 pounds up, with a top potential of 1,600 to 2,000 pounds. NMFS has established the following classifications: Small School—under

School bluefin tuna provide light-tackle trolling thrills for Henry Kong, fishing with the author and his son Mike.

27 inches curved fork length; Schools—27 inches to less than 47 inches (about 15 to 66 pounds); Large Schools—17 inches to less than 59 inches (about 66 to 135 pounds); Small Medium—59 inches to less than 73 inches (about 135 to 225 pounds); Large Medium—3 to less than 81 inches (about 225 to 315 pounds); and Giants—81 inches up.

This species is by far the largest of the tuna tribe, and the only one to which the word "giant" is applied. Though the official NMFS designation of giants starts at about 315 pounds, most anglers before regulations considered anything under 400 pounds to be a medium—and some only counted those over 500 pounds as giants.

Tuna fishing as a sport started in southern California in 1898, when a bluefin of 183 pounds was caught with the primitive tackle of the day off Catalina Island. However, the glory days of Pacific bluefin fishing are long over, a victim of intense commercial fishing. Though schoolies are still taken in fair numbers, larger bluefins are rarely seen. Prior to the 1960s, bluefins were hardly exploited along the Atlantic Coast, and the annual massive run of schoolies passed close enough to shore that the old 10-knot charter boats were able to troll them in such great numbers that the fishery was the most important of all in New Jersey and New York. A big late summer party boat tuna fishery also developed in New York Bight after World War II, but all of that became history when purse seiners (originally funded by the federal Bureau of Commercial Fisheries) destroyed the massive schools with the aid of spotter planes. The situation became critical when huge west coast purse seiners joined the slaughter for a few years during the 1960s. By the next decade the bluefin population had been reduced to less than 10 percent of what it had been, and NMFS has established ever-tougher rules which have failed to do more than stabilize the fishery at a very low level. Capture of small school bluefins in the Atlantic has been prohibited for years, and the other categories are only opened seasonally and with very low daily boat limits.

The basic problem with giant tuna is its great value as a fresh fish in Japan. Prices to more than $50 a pound have been paid to American commercial fishermen for giants shipped overnight to Tokyo. A large fleet of rod-and-reel fishermen, handliners, and harpooners follow giants in New England all summer until the annual quota established in cooperation with International Commission for the Conservation of Atlantic Tuna (ICCAT) is taken. Due to the great value involved, summer and fall sportfishing is difficult, as even rod-and-reel boats seeking giants usually fight them out of swiveling rodholders without ever taking the rod out—a clear violation of IGFA standards. Many northern giant tuna fishermen sail out of North Carolina ports from Hatteras to Morehead City for the wintering fish.

Over the years, giant tuna feeding grounds have shifted considerably. For instance, Soldier's Rip off Wedgeport, Nova Scotia once drew anglers from all over the world but has since died out, while Prince Edward Island and Canso Causeway, Nova Scotia became new hotspots for very large giants. Indeed, the world record 1,496-pounder was boated at Aulds Cove, Nova Scotia on October 26, 1979, by Ken Fraser. Bluefins of over 1,000 pounds were common at Canso Causeway for years in early November.

Bluefins can easily be confused with yellowfins and bigeyes in smaller sizes. The bluefin is distinguished by its short pectoral fins and the highest gillraker count of any tuna—34 to 43 on the first arch. The sure distinguishing feature in relation to the yellowfin is the striated liver—as compared to the yellowfin's smooth liver. The locality caught is also a good clue, as bluefins are basically inshore fish during their northerly migration whereas the other large tunas only occasionally stray far from blue waters. Giants often follow baitfish quite close to shore at such spots as Canso Causeway, and decades ago they chased menhaden schools at the mouth of Narragansett Bay, Rhode Island. Striped bass pluggers in Cape Cod Bay occasionally find themselves casting to giant boils in 20-foot depths.

School bluefins are caught both by trolling relatively short feathers, cedar jigs, and high-speed lures at seven- to nine-knot speeds and by chunking with butterfish, tinker mackerel, and other small fish. Mediums and giants are primarily taken by chunking with menhaden, butterfish, herring, mackerel and so on, or by trolling larger lures and especially spreader bars armed with mackerel or soft plastic versions of squid and mackerel.

YELLOWFIN TUNA *(Thunnus albacares)*

Range: Temperate and tropical seas worldwide.

Weight: Average 15-100 pounds, up to 400 pounds. The IGFA all-tackle record is a 405-pounder taken off Magdalena Bay, Baja Sur, Mexico by Mike Livingston in 2010.

This is the most colorful of the tunas, with all fins and finlets being golden yellow. Large yellowfins often develop overextended second dorsal and anal fins and used to be referred to as Allisons. However, marine biologists recognize those individuals as just variations of the standard yellowfin. Dead yellowfins appear similar to bluefins except for the longer pectoral fins—though the smooth liver is a positive means of identification. This excellent eating fish is favored by commercial fishermen for canning, and they're pursued by huge purse seiners in the Pacific, who take advantage of the tendency of yellowfins to feed along with dolphins. Thousands of those mammals used to be killed in the purse seining of yellowfins, but a public outcry has resulted in development of techniques that permit the release of most dolphins. Ironically, yellowfins in the Atlantic show no comparable tendency to school up with dolphins or porpoise.

The biggest yellowfins fall to anglers fishing the Revillagigedo Islands from large party boats based in San Diego. Trips of around two weeks during the winter provide opportunities to tangle with all sizes of yellowfins, though the opportunity to hook one over 200 pounds is foremost in most anglers' minds. Some over 300 pounds are boated there every winter and spring. Live baits are most popular, but the chunking technique from Atlantic waters has also proven very successful here. Many large yellowfins are trolled and taken at night on live bait off Hawaii. Yellowfins of 200 pounds are hard to come by along the Atlantic coast and in the Gulf of Mexico, but impressive numbers of smaller ones are trolled and chunked in the canyons—especially during the late-summer to fall overnight fishery from Baltimore Canyon north to Block Canyon, though anglers are now restricted by the NMFS imposition of a three yellowfin per man limit in the Atlantic and Gulf.

While yellowfins tend to stay well offshore in deep waters throughout most of their range, they do move inshore at times, with many large ones being taken during the winter just off the reef at Key West on live pilchards. Huge quantities of sand eels on lumps within 20 miles of shore drew yellowfins in from northern New Jersey to Block Island during the mid-1980s, with some being caught as close as 10 miles off Montauk. However, that hasn't happened again since.

Yellowfin tuna are colorful at any size. Bud McArthur caught this large yellowfin in Panama.

BIGEYE TUNA *(Thunnus obesus)*

Range: Atlantic coast canyons; Pacific coast from California south.

Weight: Average better than 100 pounds in the Atlantic, mostly 25-50 pounds in the Pacific except off Ecuador and Peru. The IGFA maintains separate ocean records, with the Atlantic mark being a 392-pound 6-ounce catch from the Canary Islands in 1987, while the Pacific record is 435 pounds from Cabo Blanco, Peru, in 1957.

Bigeye tuna are deepwater fish that favor cooler waters and rarely stray inshore of the canyons in the Atlantic. Though some are taken from the more southerly canyons such as Washington and Baltimore, the volume steadily increases to the north and east. These fish are almost as valuable on the Tokyo market as giant bluefins,

Bigeye tuna are tough fighters found in Mid-Atlantic and northern canyons as well as in parts of the eastern Pacific.

and longlining pressure has greatly diminished their numbers during the past few decades. The distinguishing large eye is required for the deep and primarily nocturnal feeding they favor, but bigeyes will blast to the surface at times to hit high-speed trolling lures with jetheads being the usual choice. Night chunking in the canyons also produces, though primarily on lines set deep rather than those being worked astern. Diamond jigs fished at night are also frequently effective in the canyons. Though the Pacific record is higher, that ocean is more noted for quantities of smaller bigeyes. Salinas, Ecuador often produces some very large bigeyes. Smaller bigeyes can hardly be distinguished from yellowfins, but their striated liver is a sure identifier.

ALBACORE *(Thunnus alalunga)*

Range: Temperate oceanic waters in both the Atlantic and Pacific.

Weight: Average 20-40 pounds. The IGFA record is 88 pounds 2 ounces, caught in 1977 at the Canary Islands. A 90-pounder caught off California was disqualified due to terminal tackle that didn't comply with IGFA rules.

Often simply referred to as longfin, albacore are the most important tuna on the U.S. west coast and have become increasingly significant in Atlantic canyon catches. Identification is a no-brainer, as albacore have very long pectoral fins that reach to a point aft of the anal fin. This is the white meat tuna which brings a premium price when canned, but by the same token it isn't highly regarded by the Japanese due to its lack of oil content, and consequently doesn't bring fishermen the fancy prices of bluefins, bigeyes, and large yellowfins. Marine scientists can just about predict when albacore will move within range in the Pacific by studying currents and water temperatures, which dictate their trans-Pacific migration. When schools move close to southern California an armada heads out to sea for great light-tackle action, both trolling and with live anchovies. Some years those currents carry albacore within range not only of northern California boaters but through the rest of the Pacific northwest up to southeast Alaska. On the other hand, little is known about the albacore caught in Atlantic canyons. Those fish are rarely seen in southerly canyons, but are often abundant in the Hudson and Block canyons. Most are accounted for by trolling, though some hit chunks and diamond jigs. Regardless of method, almost all are caught during the day. Atlantic albacore are also larger on average, with 50- and 60-pounders being quite common by late summer and fall. On rare occasion albacore will move inshore, and a few were caught only 10 to 15 miles from Montauk one year during the mid-1980s when sand eels also attracted yellowfins, dolphin, and white marlin inshore to 140-foot depths.

BLACKFIN TUNA *(Thunnus atlanticus)*
Range: Atlantic coast from Florida to North Carolina.
Weight: Average 10 to 25 pounds, up to about 50 pounds. The IGFA record is a 49 3/8-pounder caught at Islamorada, Florida in 2006 by Capt. Matthew E. Pullen.

The finlets of these relatively small schooling fish are uniformly dark, without

any of the yellow coloration present in other tunas. They are most abundant off the reef at Key West and on offshore humps off Marathon and Islamorada in the Florida Keys. Though relatively common during summer up to North Carolina, blackfins are rarely taken in huge quantities. They can be rather fussy at times, but will hit a variety of small trolled lures and are best chummed up with live pilchards, which provide hot feeding action that is ideal for light tackle and fly presentations.

Blackfin tuna caught at dusk on Marathon Hump from Man'O'War out of Bud'N Mary's Marina in Islamorada.

SKIPJACK TUNA *(Euthynnus pelamis)*
Range: Atlantic and Pacific temperate and tropical oceanic waters.
Weight: Average 3-15 pounds, up to perhaps 50 pounds. The IGFA all-tackle record of 45 1/4 pounds was set by Brian Evans at Flathead Bank off Baja California, in 1996.

Probably the most widely distributed and prolific member of the tunas, skipjacks are encountered in the Atlantic all the way from Cape Cod to Argentina but seem to be restricted to tropical waters in the Pacific. Formerly tagged with such oddball names as oceanic bonito and Arctic bonito, skippies aren't bonito at all but tunas that are often found in company with other tunas, especially bluefins when they move into continental shelf waters. Skipjacks are impossible to misidentify due to their "pajama pants" stripes on the belly (the only tuna with stripes below the midline) and the lack of markings on the back. They often travel in huge schools and are heavily exploited by purse seiners for lower-grade canned tuna and cat food. Most are taken

Skipjack tuna are unmistakable with their stripes on the belly.

by anglers with heavy trolling gear who are seeking larger tuna and are thus considered a nuisance. However, they're fine fighting fish on light tackle and are often targeted by small boaters when they move inshore to within 20 miles of the New Jersey and New York coasts, and can be trolled with feathers and small high-speed lures. On rare occasions they will move in much closer when blue waters are found near shore. That happened off northern New Jersey in 1999 when an angler on my boat caught a 10-pounder while casting a Hopkins into breaking fish only 200 yards offshore of Monmouth Beach, within sight of New York's skyscrapers! Later that August many more were trolled around Manasquan Ridge, which is a 50-foot lump just six miles offManasquan Inlet, New Jersey; and both a bluefin and a yellowfin were also trolled there one day on my Sheri Berri II for an inshore tuna grand slam that may never be equaled.

LITTLE TUNNY (*Euthynnus alletteratus*)

Range: Temperate and tropical Atlantic—north to Cape Cod.

Weight: Average 5-15 pounds, up to perhaps 40 pounds. The IGFA world record of 36 pounds was set at Washington Canyone off New Jersey in 2006 by Jess Lubert.

Readily identified by the scattering of black spots between the pectoral and ventral fins, little tunny also sport wavy wormlike markings on the back. Unlike most other tunas, they regularly feed close to shore and even push small baitfish right into the wash where they become a prime target for surfcasters. Little tunny is a poor name for a great gamefish, quite possibly the best of all on a pound-for-pound basis. Local names are even worse, as it's called false albacore in the Mid-Atlantic (though it

Atlantic bonito are cousins to the tunas. They primarily frequent inshore waters and are identified by the stripes on the back plus small teeth.

has a very short pectoral rather than the albacore's extended pectoral) and bonito or bonita in the South Atlantic and Gulf of Mexico—which confuses it with the real Atlantic bonito. Little tunny are favorites of inshore anglers who appreciate sport rather than eating quality. Their first run on light tackle is long and fast—and they keep repeating such runs until they literally have nothing left to give, and often die before they can be released.

Little tunny often feed on tiny baitfish and will ignore larger lures, but fly fishermen do very well with them by utilizing a fast stripping technique. Casting small jigs ahead of the breaking tunny and retrieving at high speed is very productive for spinfishermen. Trollers do well with feathers, small high-speed lures, and small spoons trolled at tuna speed (seven to nine knots). The dark, bloody meat of the little tunny is the poorest of the tuna tribe, and anglers are well advised to release them if anything better is available. Those wishing to try little tunny should bleed them immediately, fillet as soon as possible, and then soak the meat in brine (clean salt water with ice). Little tunny make great live baits for blue marlin, and are also prized for use in making belly strip trolling baits. A similar species found in the tropical eastern Pacific is the black skipjack *(Euthynnus lineatus),* which is the prime live bait for black marlin, while the kawakawa *(Euthynnus affinis)* fills the same niche in the western Pacific.

ATLANTIC BONITO *(Sarda sarda)*

Range: Atlantic coast from Cape Cod south, though not common much below New Jersey.

Weight: Average 3-7 pounds, up to 20 pounds. The IGFA record is 18 1/4 pounds from the Azores in 1953.

Bonito are closely related to the tunas and often mix with them. They differ in appearance from tuna in that they have stripes on the back and the mouth is full of tiny, sharp teeth which, fortunately, do little damage to mono leaders. A fine fighting fish, the bonito will readily take small leadhead and diamond jigs retrieved at a fast rate and with lots of sharp jigging. They also can be chummed with small baitfish such as spearing and respond to small trolled lures but especially tiny spoons fished under the surface with drails or by using wire line or downriggers. Their light-colored meat is of excellent quality.

PACIFIC BONITO *(Sarda chiliensis lineolatus)*

Range: Primarily California and Baja California.

Size: Average 2-5 pounds. Possibly to 20 pounds. The IGFA record is 14 3/4 pounds caught off San Benitos Island, Baja California, in 1980 by Jerome Rilling.

There are two other closely-related species caught in other parts of the Pacific, but this is an important sport and food fish for California anglers, particularly those fishing from party boats in southern California.

Author battles a shark in the Gulf of Mexico off Marco, Florida.

SHARKS

These ancient creatures have remained almost unchanged and undiminished for ages, but have shown signs of vulnerability in recent years due to a huge increase in commercial fishing primarily to supply fins to the Orient for high prices. Though the meat is also of some value, there is so much more money involved in fins that many commercial fishermen were simply cutting the fins off live sharks and dumping the fish back to die instead of taking up hold space with the carcasses. That practice has been outlawed in U.S. Atlantic, Caribbean, and Gulf of Mexico waters, and also in Hawaii, but will probably continue in many other areas of the world. Little was known about sharks until recent decades, but tagging programs started by Jack Casey for NMFS and carried out primarily by volunteer sportfishermen have established migratory patterns and given an indication of growth rates. Sharks are slow-growing, long-lived fish with low reproductive capacity. While they thrive in temperate and tropical waters worldwide, wherever commercial fisheries have been developed for them (even in remote areas) their numbers have quickly been diminished to the point where the venture is no longer viable. Sportfishing has been affected by that increased pressure in many areas, and management is necessary to prevent the crash of many species that cannot be brought back quickly with strict measures, as is the case with bony fish. Sharks are quite different from other fish in that they have cartilage rather than bones, and carry nitrogen in the blood stream, which creates an unpleasant odor after death.

Any sharks desired for food should be bled immediately and cleaned as soon as possible. Sharks also have five to seven paired gill openings on the sides of the head, as compared to just one pair in bony fishes, and their skin has a sandpaper texture due to being covered with minute toothlike scales. Rub a shark from head to tail and it feels smooth as silk, but go the other way and your hand is shredded. Though rather primitive, sharks have at least one evolutionary advantage on man. Their teeth are expendable, as new ones are lined up in the jaws ready to move forward as one is lost.

SHORTFIN MAKO SHARK *(Isurus oxyrinchus)*

Range: Worldwide in temperate and tropical seas.

Weight: Average 50-200 pounds, up to 1,200 pounds or more. The IGFA world record is 1,221 pounds taken in 2001 off Chatham, Massachusetts by Luke Sweeney.

This is the most prized of all sharks and the one which the sportfishery from Virginia to New England concentrates on. There's no mistaking a mako, as the fish sports a mouth full of long sharp teeth that protrude but which are curved inward. The body is fairly compact (an eight-footer should weigh about 400 pounds) and quite colorful, with a blue back. Makos are a true gamefish, providing the most spectacular leaps of all. Those jumps are unpredictable, as the line is usually heading in one direction when the mako emerges far to the right or left as if it were another fish altogether. The typical jump is usually straight up, perhaps 20 feet in the air, at which point the mako flips around to head back in nose first. Makos also fight hard (a 975-pound state record caught in 2000 on the Reelistic from Indian River, Delaware, was fought on heavy stand-up tackle with 130-pound mono for 14 hours) and are excellent eating fish with steaks similar in appearance and flavor to swordfish. The usual method of catching makos is by drifting baits into chum lines. However, trolling heavy lures with baits attached is very productive for California anglers. Though makos are oceanic sharks, they do move inshore in the Atlantic after their favorite food—bluefish. Party boats fishing at night only a few miles off New Jersey and Long Island often see makos slide into the slick. With longliners catching large quantities of these prized and increasingly valuable sharks, it's amazing there are any left at all, as males don't mature until they're around 250 pounds and females until they're about 600 pounds, which is an exceptionally large size to be caught by any means. Furthermore, only a few pregnant females have ever been inspected worldwide!

The very similar longfin mako *(Isurus paucus)* is a deepwater cousin of the Atlantic and Gulf of Mexico, which is rarely encountered by anglers but often taken on longlines. That is one of several deep-sea sharks that have been placed on the prohibited-to-land list by NMFS.

PORBEAGLE SHARK *(Lamna nasus)*

Range: Cool temperate waters of the Atlantic. Also found in the Mediterranean and the southern Pacific.

Weight: Average 100-400 pounds, up to 600 pounds or more. The IGFA record is 507 pounds set in 1993 at Pentland Firth, Caithness, Scotland.

This fine gamefish is closely related to the mako, but prefers much cooler waters. In the U.S. it is caught almost exclusively in New England waters. A few were taken off the south shore of Long Island during the early days of sport sharking in the 1960s, but Cox's Ledge (about 40 miles east of Montauk) is the most westerly area from which porbeagles have been reported in decades. These sharks were longlined by fishermen from Cape Verde Islands long before there was much general interest in sharks as food, and they appeared to make a big dent in the American population. Though a mako look-alike, it has very different teeth that are smooth, with small cusps on both sides at the base. There's also a distinguishing white patch at the base of the first dorsal fin.

WHITE SHARK *(Carcharodon carcharias)*

Range: Worldwide in temperate and tropical waters. Most common in slightly cooler areas such as off San Francisco and from New Jersey to Maine.

Weight: Average 200-1,000 pounds, up to several tons. The IGFA all-tackle record is a 2,664-pounder taken in 1959 by Alfred Dean at Ceduna, South Australia.

Part of the same family as the mako and porbeagle, the white is a bigger, lazier, and more dangerous shark that seems to prefer mammals rather than fish as it grows older. Thus, the frequent reference to whites as man-eaters has some validity, though it's unlikely they single out human beings as prey. Seals and sea lions are regular items on their menus, which is why they're most likely to be encountered in waters around San Francisco and similar areas. Divers resemble their prey, although in most recorded instances whites spit out the humans they attacked after apparently realizing their error. Fossil teeth prove this shark grew much larger in previous ages, but they still attain weights of several tons. Ironically, the "man-eater" is one of the few sharks protected completely by NMFS, and none may be landed. Whites don't reach sexual maturity until 11 to 14 feet in length, which may account for their small numbers. Relatively common only around concentrations of seals, the sighting of a white by even veteran northeast U.S. shark fishermen is a rarity, though the appearance of a large dead whale floating offshore will almost invariably result in a gathering of several whites to feed on the putrid carcass. It was from such a whale that angler Donnie Braddick and famed shark hunter Capt. Frank Mundus extracted a 3,427-pounder on rod and reel before there were any catch restrictions. The IGFA didn't recognize that catch because a mammal (the whale) was literally being used as chum, which is prohibited. Though partially warm-blooded, as are the other mackerel sharks, the white is not a great fighter like the mako and porbeagle.

BLUE SHARK *(Prioace glauca)*

Range: Worldwide in temperate seas.

Weight: Average 50-200 pounds, up to perhaps 500 pounds. The IGFA world record is a 528-pounder caught in 2001 in Montauk, New York by Joe Seidel.

Blues are the most abundant of sharks in temperate waters such as those found off California and from New Jersey to Maine. Longline fishermen all the way out to the Grand Banks and Flemish Cap often find their lines loaded with blues of all sizes. These are the dumbest of fish, often returning to take a hook again after being released. I've caught the same blue three times within two hours of drifting, and tagged blues are regularly taken within a day or two of when and where they were released. They're

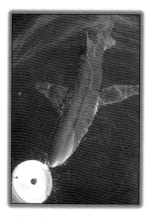

Blue sharks are curious and will usually come right to the boat, as this one is poking the chum pot.

not fighters in the class of makos or many other sharks, but are good sport on appropriately light tackle since they tend to stay on the surface and can be overcome with practically any sort of gear. They aren't line shy and can frequently be chummed right to the boat to be baited with appropriate tackle. Flyrod fishermen particularly like blues as they readily suck in flies. While other sharks are being depleted by longlining, blues remain fairly abundant since their watery flesh is not desirable and almost all are released by sportfishermen. Blues are oceanic sharks, but they do move inshore to 10 miles or so in some areas to the northeast. They show up in May off New Jersey when water temperatures are only in the mid-50s and may be caught well into the fall.

THRESHER SHARK *(Alopias vulpinus)*

Range: Worldwide in cool temperate waters such as found in the Atlantic from New Jersey north, and off southern California.

Weight: Average 200-500 pounds. The IGFA world record of 767 pounds 3 ounces was caught at Bay of Islands, New Zealand, in 1983 by D. L. Hannah.

The longtail thresher referred to here is the common worldwide species, though there's also the pelagic thresher of the Pacific and both Atlantic and Pacific bigeye threshers. The latter live in deep offshore waters and are rarely caught by sportsmen. Threshers rank with makos as the greatest gamefish of the shark family, but have relatively small mouths with small teeth. Their distinguishing feature is the upper lobe of the tail, which is longer than the rest of the body. That tail is used to stun baitfish so the thresher can pick up his meal at leisure. These very strong fighters may also jump, and their thrashing tail makes them a dangerous fish to deal with at boatside. Threshers are very good eating, a factor which has led to their decline in California due to heavy commercial fishing. On the other hand, threshers seem to be more abundant in recent years along the east coast

Thresher sharks are immediately identified by the long tail.

from New Jersey to Martha's Vineyard, and they've actually become common feeding inshore on schools of menhaden—often within a mile of New Jersey and Long Island beaches, though they're still an unusual catch for sharkers.

TIGER SHARK *(Galeocerdo cuvieri)*

Range: Worldwide in temperate and tropical seas. Common along the Atlantic coast from Florida to southern New England.

Weight: Average 200-500 pounds, to over 2,000 pounds. The IGFA record is 1,780 pounds caught from a pier at Cherry Grove, South Carolina, in 1964 by Walter Maxwell.

Though one of the largest of sharks, the tiger doesn't rank highly as a sportfish. It tends to act more like a bottomfish than a pelagic wanderer when hooked, and is easily subdued on heavy tackle. The tiger stripes are a dead giveaway in smaller tigers, but those marks tend to fade as the fish grows larger. The teeth provide instant recognition as they are cockscomb-shaped with serrated edges. Tigers are noted for eating just about anything, and all manner of bird and beast have been removed from their stomachs, along with many inanimate objects. That lack of discrimination has also earned them a reputation as man-eaters.

Tiger sharks get large, and this 605-pounder won the New Jersey Coast Shark Anglers High Rollers Tournament for Mike Koblan while fishing from the author's center console Sherri Berri II.

HAMMERHEAD SHARKS *(Family Sphyrnidae)*

Range: Warm temperate and tropical waters worldwide.

Weight: Varies with species. The great hammerhead grows to 20 feet and well over 1,000 pounds. The IGFA record is 1,280 pounds caught in 2006 at Boca Grande, Florida by Bucky Dennis. The scalloped hammerhead record is 353 pounds caught at Key West, Florida, in 2004 by Rick Gunion, while the smooth hammerhead mark is 369 pounds 7 ounces taken at Bay of Plenty, New Zealand, in 2002 by Scott Tindale.

Hammerhead sharks are immediately identified by their unique head, in which the eyes are located at the ends of two thin protrusions resembling a hammer. Only the most observant are aware there are three major species as well as minor ones. The great hammerhead *(Sphyrna mokarran)* is by far the largest and the most tropical, rarely being seen off the mid-Atlantic coast even during midsummer. This is a dangerous and very aggressive shark, which may not have teeth as large as others but which uses them to great advantage in attacking large prey such as rays. It has a T-shaped head that is notched in the center. The scalloped hammerhead *(Sphyrna lewini)* reaches 10 feet and has a head which is rounded and notched. The smooth hammerhead *(Sphyrna zygaena),* which is most often encountered close to shore,

grows to 14 feet and has a rounded head that is unnotched. Hammerheads are surprisingly strong fighters, though sportfishermen rarely seek them. Those that migrate north during summer are often seen swimming on the surface and are easily approached but will rarely strike anything. Even those attracted to chum slicks are often difficult to fool. A much smaller member of the family is the similar-looking bonnethead *(Sphyrna tiburo),* which sports a very short-lobed, shovel-shaped head. Bonnetheads are common on the Florida Keys flats and put up a good battle on light tackle. Most weigh only a few pounds, but the IGFA record is a 23-pound 11-ounce specimen caught by Chad Wood at Cumberland Sound, Georgia, in 1994.

Though the teeth of the scalloped ham-merhead are small, these sharks can be very aggressive and are excellent fighters.

SANDBAR SHARK *(Carcharhinus milberti)*

Range: Temperate waters of the Atlantic and Gulf of Mexico.

Weight: Average 30 -100 pounds. Up to 150 pounds or more. The IGFA world record is 529 pounds 1 ounce by Patrick Sebile at Guinea-Bissau in 2002.

Sandbar sharks used to be very abundant over inshore waters of the Atlantic continental shelf until commercial fishermen targeted them for their fins, which are used in the Orient to make shark fin soup. Sandbars are also one of the best eating sharks. They are much better known as "browns" and are fine fighters for their size. Sandbars spawn in bays, and the pups are

Sandbar (brown) shark alongside with tag implanted.

often encountered there by bottom-fishermen who think they have a dogfish until the small, sharp teeth become visible. They're distinguished from the similar, but much larger, dusky by the larger first dorsal fin, which is also farther forward in relation to the pectoral fins. Browns are very slow growing and take about 15 years to mature. One I tagged off Montauk at about 40 pounds was recovered eight years later off Mexico and had only doubled in size.

DUSKY SHARK *(Carcharhinus obscurus)*

Range: Temperate waters.

Weight: Average 200-500 pounds. The IGFA record is 764 pounds set at Longboat Key, Florida, in 1982 by Warren Girle.

The dusky is a big, often lazy, shark that looks almost like the sandbar but grows much larger. It's become almost rare after intensive commercial fishing for its fins reduced the population to a fraction of what it had been. The NMFS has placed the dusky on its prohibited list, and they may no longer be landed.

BLACKTIP SHARK *(Carcharhinus limbatus)*

Range: Tropical Atlantic and Gulf of Mexico.

Weight: Average 50-100 pounds. The IGFA record is 270 pounds 9 ounces from Malindi Bay, Kenya, in 1984.

Distinguished by the black tips of its fins, the blacktip is probably the most popular inshore shark in Florida and the Gulf of Mexico. It is very aggressive and will hit lures

Blacktip sharks are aggressive enough to hit lures, often jump, and can inflict nasty wounds, if not handled carefully.

on the flats, though anglers must be sure to draw the lure right by the shark's nose so he can see it. Once hooked, blacktips usually take to the air and provide sizzling runs on light tackle. They're excellent eating, which has become a problem with the increase in commercial sharking.

SPINNER SHARK (*Carcharhinus brevipinna*)

Range: Tropical Atlantic and Gulf of Mexico.

Weight: Average 50-100 pounds. The IGFA record is 208 pounds and 9 ounces caught at Port Aransas, Texas in 2009 by Raymond Ireton.

Very similar to blacktips and often found in the same areas, spinners are great jumpers and fight hard on appropriate tackle.

LEMON SHARK (*Negaprion brevirostris*)

Range: Tropical and semi-tropical Atlantic, Caribbean, and Gulf of Mexico.

Weight: Average 50-100 pounds. The IGFA record is 405 pounds from Buxton, North Carolina, caught in 1988 by Colleen D. Harlow.

This yellowish-brown, blunt-snouted shark has two triangular dorsal fins that are nearly the same size. Lemons are another shallow-water shark frequently encountered on the flats in the Florida Keys and the Bahamas. They respond to lures and are good fighters, though not as spectacular as blacktips and spinners.

BULL SHARK (*Carcharhinus leucas*)

Range: Worldwide in tropical and semi-tropical waters.

Weight: Average 100-200 pounds. The IGFA record is 697 3/4 pounds from Malindi, Kenya, in 2001 by Ronald de Jager.

This may well be the most vicious and dangerous of sharks since it favors shallow, discolored waters and will strike at anything thrashing around, including swimmers. Bulls are abundant around rivermouths in the Gulf of Mexico and Caribbean, and many natives in Latin America won't go swimming because their presence isn't limited to salt water. Bulls swim inside the rivers and lagoons, and have become landlocked in Lake Nicaragua, where they've established a reputation as man-eaters. The bull is an undistinguished-looking shark with a short, broadly rounded snout, a large dorsal fin that is far forward, sub-triangular serrated teeth, and no ridge on the back between the dorsal fins. Though they have a reputation as poor fighters, bulls will hit lures on the flats and are good sport for light-tackle anglers.

SAND TIGER SHARK (*Odontaspis taurus*)

Range: Atlantic temperate waters.

Weight: Average 50-200 pounds. The IGFA record is 350 pounds 2 ounces caught by Mark Thawley in 1993 at Charleston Jetty, South Carolina.

The sand tiger is the most misleading of all sharks as it sports a mouthful of wicked teeth similar to those of a mako but is actually an innocuous bottom feeder. These are ideal sharks for aquariums due to their fierce look and the ease of maintaining them. They seem to be most abundant in Delaware Bay, and there was once a substantial sportfishery for them there, though they aren't normally good fighters. However, sand tigers are now on the NMFS prohibited list after years of overexploitation.

ATLANTIC SHARPNOSE *(Rhizoprionodon terraenovae)*
Range: Tropical and semi-tropical Atlantic, Gulf of Mexico, and Caribbean.
Weight: Average 5-10 pounds. The IGFA record is 16 pounds from Port Mansfield, Texas, in 1994 by R. Bruce Shields.

This small, shallow-water member of the requiem shark family is an important sport and food fish in the Gulf of Mexico. It's distinguished by smooth-edged curved teeth and the presence of well-developed labial furrows around the corners of its mouth.

SMOOTH DOGFISH *(Mustelus canis)*
Range: Atlantic and Gulf coasts.
Weight: Average 3-10 pounds. The IGFA record is 37 1/2 pounds caught at Cape May, New Jersey, in 2007 by David Spletzer.

This small shark is a warmwater species often referred to as sand shark. However, dogfish only have grinder teeth, and this species is easy to handle. No one fishes for them, but anglers drifting for summer flounder hook into dogfish regularly and often figure they've hooked a "doormat." Like other sharks they're good-eating if bled and cleaned promptly.

Smooth dogfish are an inshore Mid-Atlantic species that often surprise fluke anglers—in this case, Cyndi Ristori.

SPINY DOGFISH *(Squalus acanthis)*
Range: North Carolina to Canada.
Weight: Average 3-12 pounds. The IGFA record is 15 3/4 pounds from Kenmare Bay, Co. Kerry, Ireland, in 1989.

Like its summer relative, the spiny dogfish only has grinder teeth—but it injures many more fishermen than any other shark with the sharp spine located behind the

Spiny dogfish are born alive, as is the case with almost all sharks, and this one swam away even with the placenta still attached. Note the spines behind the dorsal fins which easily puncture hands.

dorsal fins. Not only do those spines easily penetrate flesh, but they frequently cause infections. As a result, anglers generally avoid them, though that's not always easy to do when these cold water sharks start migrating toward shore as waters cool in fall. Though basically bottomfish, they'll even rise up in the water column to grab baits intended for bluefin tuna by chunkers. Spiny dogfish are the basic ingredient in the famed English fish and chips, and with European populations overfished American dogfish have been targeted for export. The resulting commercial concentration has quickly reduced those stocks. That is especially true with the larger females, which absorbed the brunt of the commercial fishery. The NMFS has stepped in with a strict management plan to stabilize the fishery.

WARM WATER SPECIES

Following are the most important species found primarily in warmer waters from Cape Hatteras south to the Caribbean and into the Gulf of Mexico, plus Hawaii and the eastern Pacific south of California. Almost all are inshore fish, but a few oceanic fish that don't fit into the families already described are also included. Many Atlantic species at least occasionally move farther north, even as far as Cape Cod, during late summer when waters are warmest. Several species even used to be common to the north over a century ago, and some still remain abundant in Chesapeake and Delaware bays.

DOLPHIN *(Coryphaena hippurus)*

Range: Worldwide in temperate and tropical offshore waters.

Weight: Average 2-30 pounds. The IGFA record is 87 pounds by Manuel Salazar at Papagallo Gulf, Costa Rica in 1976.

Probably the most beautiful species in the oceans, this world traveler displays a greenish-blue or yellow appearance and may also show dark vertical bands when excited. However, upon dying that color becomes drab. There's no mistaking this species for any other except the small, roundish pompano dolphin *(Coryphaena equisetis)* which only grows to about five pounds and is more common far to sea. The dolphin name is so well established that the American Fisheries Society hasn't changed it despite the confusion with the mammal of the same name. Even though the Spanish name, dorado (gold), is very descriptive, it too is shared with a freshwater gamefish found in Argentina and Paraguay. As a result, the Hawaiian name, mahi-mahi, has become popular and is most frequently used in restaurants where this excellent-eating fish is very popular.

Dolphin are beautiful fish and great fighters at any size.

Dolphin are unique in the largely unisex fish kingdom in that the sexes can be readily identified in all but the smallest sizes. Males sport a very blunt forehead and, also unlike most species, they grow larger than females. While smaller dolphin often form large schools, large adults are frequently encountered in male/female pairs and anglers are always on the alert for a follower behind a hooked dolphin.

Dolphin are great gamefish, combining speed and endurance with spectacular leaps. They're among the fastest growing of all species, attain great sizes in a mere few years of life, and are frequently associated with floating debris or rafts of sagassum weed which concentrate the small fish they feed upon. Though found in warm waters year-round, dolphin also display migratory patterns such as the one which carries them from the Florida Keys during the spring up the Atlantic Coast. While primarily an offshore species, they frequently wander into shallower areas especially when warm, blue waters spread inshore.

Dolphin will hit a variety of lures and baits in all sizes, but particularly like balao and flying fish. Their delicate flesh is delicious, but must be kept cool and doesn't stand up to long periods of freezing. The leathery skin is usually stripped off before filleting.

MACKERELS *(Scombridae)*

These streamlined and exceptionally fast fish are mostly semi-tropical in nature, though the smaller but very important Atlantic mackerel will be covered in the next section on primarily northern species. All sport very sharp eyesight and are rarely fooled by slow-moving lures. Except when using live baits, trolling for these mackerels is normally done at tuna speeds.

WAHOO *(Acanthocybium solanderi)*

Range: Worldwide in tropical and semi-tropical waters.

Weight: Average 10-60 pounds. The IGFA record is 184 pounds caught by Sara Hayward at Cabo San Lucas in 2005.

This oceanic species is among the most colorful of all when alive, as it displays vertical black bars along its sides. It may well be the fastest of all fish, and displays an uncanny ability to be able to slice a bait directly behind wherever the hook is placed even while hitting it at high speed. The first run of a hooked wahoo is among the most exciting in fishing, but as long as there's some line left on the reel the fight after that point is usually much easier.

Wahoo are among the most colorful of oceanic fish and possibly the fastest. This one was gaffed by Capt. Roger Aleong off Trinidad's north coast.

The wahoo's mouthful of small but very sharp teeth can slice through just about anything except wire, and they can do so with such efficiency that a bait is often cut in two without the line ever being popped out of the outrigger pin. Though wahoo don't jump when hooked, they occasionally make spectacular high, arching leaps to pounce on baits. These oceanic wanderers don't seem to school in the Atlantic, but do tend to aggregate in areas at certain times of year. The largest of all are encountered during winter and early spring off the southern Bahamas, where specimens over 100 pounds are common. Trinidad's north coast is also noted for its winter wahoo run, and significant numbers are encountered off Hatteras in the spring and throughout the canyons up to Long Island during summer. Schooling is more common in the Pacific where large numbers of wahoo can be caught during the rainy season. During one December trip, I was able to hook them on every pass within yards of shore off the famous Wahoo Rock near Isla Coiba, Panama. However, as is the case in the Bahamas, many of those wahoo are lost to sharks which would never be able to catch them if they weren't hooked. There's little liklihood of being able to troll too fast for a wahoo to catch up to a bait or lure, and Bahamas pros such as Capt. Ron Schatman developed a system of trolling at 18 knots for that species. In many cases wahoo are hooked more consistently with lures and baits run deeper by using wire line or downriggers. Wahoo are generally considered to be among the best-eating of all fish.

KING MACKEREL *(Scomberomorus cavalla)*
Range: Widespread inshore in the Atlantic Ocean (especially from Virginia south), Caribbean Sea, and Gulf of Mexico.
Weight: Average 5-50 pounds. The IGFA record is 93 pounds caught by Steve Perez Graulau at San Juan, Puerto Rico in 1999.

King mackerel are the largest of the inshore mackerels, and the focus of a big money tournament circuit. Capt. Robert Trosset holds a king before release off Key West for Cam Smith-Arnold of Suzuki.

Usually referred to as kingfish, this is the most popular of the inshore mackerels as it's often found in large schools but also grows to substantial sizes. Like the wahoo, it supplies a blistering first run but rarely fights very long after that. Heavily impacted by purse seining and gillnetting, this formerly superabundant species has been brought back by management plans adopted by the South Atlantic and Gulf Fishery Management Councils and is once again among the most popular sport and food fishes from North Carolina to Texas. The silvery-green king is the least colorful of the warmwater mackerels, as it has small yellow spots only as a juvenile. These fade as it grows larger, but the sure sign of the species is the sharp dip in the lateral line under the second dorsal fin.

There are two major migratory groups: one that moves from southeast Florida north along the coast, and another that travels from southwest Florida to Louisiana and Texas, where anglers seek them around oil rigs and anchored shrimp boats. Kings even move inshore to piers and jetties at times, and will hit a variety of fast-moving lures plus live and dead baits. Spoons are very effective, and smaller schooling kings are suckers for live pilchards. Large kings ("smokers") prefer bigger live baits such as grunts and Lane snappers on the Florida reefs and menhaden off the North Carolina Outer Banks in the fall. Kings are a popular restaurant fish, and are normally cut into steaks.

SPANISH MACKEREL *(Scomberomorus maculatus)*
Range: Atlantic from Long Island south, plus Caribbean and Gulf of Mexico.
Weight: Average 1-5 pounds. The IGFA record is 13 pounds caught by Robert Cranton at Ocracoke Inlet, North Carolina, in 1987.

The smallest of the warmwater mackerels is also the most common in inshore waters. It's a favorite of small boaters both along the coast and within bays—and also provides action for surfcasters. Though primarily a southern fish, it's found in fair quantities almost every summer in New York Bight. Like the king mackerel, it was

Spanish mackerel are primarily a southern inshore species, but are common up to New York during late summer.

severely over-fished by netters before coming under regulation by the South Atlantic and Gulf Fishery Management Councils, which have been successful in restoring significant populations of a species that was historically superabundant. Spanish mackerel are slim fish with roundish yellow spots on the sides that aren't arranged in a row, as with the cero mackerel. They can be confused with king mackerel only at the smallest sizes when kings still have spots, but Spanish lack the sharp dip in the lateral line below the second dorsal fin. Often encountered in large schools, Spanish mackerel will readily hit a variety of small jigs, feathers, and spoons retrieved or trolled at high speed. Very light wire leaders are important in order to save lures while not alerting the sharp-eyed mackerel. Though somewhat oily, Spanish mackerel are good eating fish especially when fresh.

CERO MACKEREL *(Scomberomorus regalis)*
Range: South Atlantic coast.
Weight: Average 5-10 pounds. The IGFA record is 17 1/8 pounds caught by G. Michael Mills at Islamorada, Florida Keys, in 1986.

Far less common than Spanish or king mackerel, the cero is more of a loner and usually found farther off on the reef. It also rarely ranges far north into the Gulf of Mexico or much beyond Florida on the Atlantic. Though somewhat similar to the Spanish, ceros have elongated, rather than roundish, yellow spots and also a prominent straight yellow line along the midsection. They average larger than Spanish but never attain the size of kings.

Cero mackerel, such as this one held by Capt. Joe Alexander during a rough day off Key West, are separated from kings and Spanish mackerel by the straight line down their sides.

JACKS *(Carangidae)*

When it comes to fighting qualities, I rate the jacks just a step below the tunas and billfish. Many are certainly among the toughest species and display exceptional endurance on light tackle, but only the roosterfish ordinarily jumps when hooked.

Many jacks also have dark, strong-tasting flesh, and some of the larger species have been implicated in ciguatera poisoning in tropical areas where that problem is present. Yet, also among the 140 or so members of this family, with members found throughout the world's warm waters, are such outstanding eating fish as the pompano. Many jacks have broad bodies that are covered in very small scales which, at the end of the lateral line, are enlarged to form a keel. Those large scales, or scutes, are rough to the touch.

GREATER AMBERJACK *(Seriola dumerili)*

Range: Almost worldwide, in tropical and warm, temperate waters.

Weight: Average 10-60 pounds. The IGFA record is 156 pounds 13 ounces by Hideyuki Nemoto at Iki Island, Japan in 2010.

The largest of the jacks is more streamlined than most, but is still a heavy-bodied fish. The very largest specimens are almost impossible to move from their deepwater haunts, and may be eaten by sharks before they can be brought to the surface even on heavy tackle. This Atlantic and Gulf of Mexico species used to be considered virtually inedible due to the frequency of infestation with harmless, but unappetizing worms. That fact kept them abundant until recently on deepwater wrecks and humps off southeast Florida, but commercial fishing finally got to them as raw material for fast food fish sandwiches, despite the low yield. As a result, charter skippers can no longer count on bailing out a tough day by dropping a chunk of bait to bottom, where it used to be almost impossible to get through the massive schools of amberjack without hooking up. Now live baits (such as grunts) are almost a must. Limits and closed seasons are now in place to save this great gamefish, which can be caught even from 200- and 300-foot depths on relatively light tackle by skilled anglers. A very similar Atlantic species is the almaco jack *(Seriola rivoliana)* which is usually much smaller (about 5 to 20 pounds) but has been caught up to 78 pounds at Argus Bank, Bermuda. The IGFA also lists a Pacific almaco under the same scientific name, with a record of 132 pounds from La Paz, Baja California, in 1964.

Amberjack develop a black "feeding stripe" through the eye when excited. Gene Graman holds a typical Key West amberjack.

49

The Pacific amberjack *(Seriola colburni)* grows just as large as the greater amberjack and doesn't have the worm problem. It's found in the eastern Pacific from Baja California south and is highly regarded as a food fish.

Amberjack identification is simple except when they're juveniles and sport five body bands. Though the color can vary, they're basically dark above and lighter along the sides. A black stripe from the upper jaw through the eye to the top of the head becomes prominent in excited amberjack, as does an amber band from the eyes to the tail. These migratory fish are very abundant off southeast Florida during the winter, but spread north to Virginia and into the northern Gulf of Mexico in spring. In addition to frequenting wrecks, they're commonly found around offshore buoys and oil rigs. They're suckers for live baits, and often go crazy over popping plugs in shallower waters. Flyfishermen do best after teasing amberjack close to the boat with live baits.

CREVALLE JACK *(Caranx hippos)*

Range: Western Atlantic shores from Virginia south, Gulf of Mexico, and Caribbean Sea.

Weight: Average 2-20 pounds. The IGFA record is 66 1/8 pounds from Barra Do Dande, Angola by Carlos Alberto Leal Simoes in 2010.

More frequently referred to as jack crevalle (cavalli in Trinidad), this may be the toughest of all shallow-water fish and many anglers fear hooking them on light tackle as the fight may go on for an hour just to release a 10- to 15-pounder.

Crevalle jack, more commonly called jack crevalle, are among the toughest fighters on light tackle.

They're identified by the blunt forehead and black spots on the edge of the gill covers and the pectoral fin. These extremely aggressive jacks feed in schools when small, but tend to become loners when they get larger. They'll readily hit popping plugs and fast-retrieved lures of many types, as well as live baits. A similar species *(Caranx caninus)* is found along tropical Pacific shores but doesn't seem to grow quite as large. The Pacific crevalle jack record is 39 pounds from Playa Zancudo, Costa Rica, by Ingrid Callaghan in 1997.

HORSE-EYE JACK *(Caranx latus)*

Range: Tropical Atlantic.

Weight: Average 2-15 pounds. The IGFA record is 29 1/2 pounds taken in 1993 from Ascension Island in the South Atlantic.

Horse-eye jacks are the abundant inshore jack in the Bahamas. This one was a record at Walker's Cay. They're most frequently caught at night in Florida.

Very similar to the crevalle jack, the horse-eye is only an occasional catch in Florida (primarily at night) but is the abundant jack in the Bahamas, where they are frequently associated with ciguatera poisoning. Horse-eyes are blander-looking and don't seem to get quite as large as crevalles, but are strong fighters. The similar tropical Pacific species is the bigeye trevally *(Caranx sexfasciatus),* which is abundant in Panama, averages the same size, and is also most active at night. The record is 31 1/2 pounds from Poivre Island, Seychelles, in 1997.

BLUE RUNNER *(Caranx crysos)*

Range: Atlantic from Long Island south, Gulf of Mexico, and Caribbean Sea.

Weight: Average: 1/2 to 2 pounds. The IGFA record is 11 1/8 pounds from Dauphin Island, Alabama, by Stacey Michele Moiren in 1997.

Though usually looked down on as a baitfish, the blue runner provides excellent sport on light tackle as well as being a prime live bait for large predators such as cobia, amberjack, barracuda, and sailfish. They'll hit a wide variety of small jigs and spoons, and frequently tear apart Sabiki bait jigging rigs. Blue runners are more slender in profile than other jacks, and have a small black spot on the gill cover.

Blue runners are usually less than a pound and most often used as bait, but they do grow much larger, as is the case with this one from Walker's Cay, Bahamas.

AFRICAN POMPANO *(Alectis cilaris)*

Range: Almost worldwide in tropical waters.

Weight: Average 10-30 pounds. The IGFA record is 50 1/2 pounds from Daytona Beach, Florida, by Tom Sargent in 1990.

African pompano sport long filiments off their fins when young.

Near-record African pompano such as this 42 1/2-pounder trolled off Palm Beach by the author in 1969, show no trace of those filaments.

This is one of the most fascinating fish in that the young bear little resemblence to adults. Juvenile African pompano appear almost unreal with thread-like rays protruding from their dorsal and anal fins that are up to four times longer than their body. As the fish grows, those rays shorten and eventually disappear, leaving a slab-sided silvery fish with a very steep forehead. Though not abundant anywhere, Africans are taken regularly off Florida's southeast coast and in the Keys, with live baits accounting for most of the catches. Though just as tough a fighter as the other jacks, the African rates much higher on the plate. A very similar species is found in the tropical Pacific, where I even caught one at remote Christmas Island.

FLORIDA POMPANO *(Trachinotus carolinus)*
Range: North Carolina to Florida and Gulf of Mexico.
Weight: Average 1-2 pounds. The IGFA record is 8 1/4 pounds from Port St. Joe Bay, Florida by Barry Huston in 1999.

The gourmet's delight is a common Florida inshore species that has increased in abundance since gill-netting was outlawed in that state. Though they are fine game-

Pompano are a gourmet's delight and a favorite of Florida surfcasters. Cyndi Ristori displays her catch north of Jupiter.

fish, most are caught on heavy surfcasting tackle required for casting rigs to the outer bars. Sand fleas are the usual bait along the southeast Florida coast, though clams are favored on the central coast. Pompano range well north in the summer and are reasonably abundant along the Outer Banks of North Carolina. In addition to the surf, many pompano are caught in southern inlets, bays, and around bridges where they frequently hit small jigs—as is also the case at shallow Gulf oil rigs. The golden-hued pompano is easy to identify. The similarly-shaped palometa *(Trachinotus goodei)* is also known as the long-finned pompano and sports four to five narrow vertical bars on the sides, plus very long dorsal and anal fins. It's a small fish more common in the Bermuda surf.

PERMIT *(Trachinotus falcatus)*
Range: Florida, Bahamas, Mexico, and some Caribbean islands.

Weight: Average 5-25 pounds. The IGFA record is 60 pounds from Ilha do Mel, Paranagua, Brazil by Renato Fiedler in 2002.

The only fish the pompano can be confused with is a young permit. These fish are the greatest prize for flats anglers and have a somewhat deeper body. Though casting to them on the flats is the most exciting form of the sport, permit are easier to hook in other ways. They usually bite readily when found circling shallow wrecks in the western Gulf of Mexico, as well as on reefs and in Key West Harbor. Chumming with shrimp boat "trash" crabs is the key to getting them interested and they'll often eat those dead crabs on a hook or jig, though small live crabs are the deadliest bait. Stray permit, including some of the largest, are often caught from Florida east coast piers and in the surf. Permit are powerful fighters

Permit are the most challenging flats species. The author prepares to release this one in the mid-30s after catching it with Capt. Harlan Franklin in the "lakes" west of Key West.

on light tackle and are almost always released, though their flesh is comparable to that of the pompano.

LOOKDOWN *(Selene vomer)*
Range: Tropical inshore waters.
Weight: Average 1/2 to 1 pound. The IGFA record is 4 3/4 pounds from Flamingo, Florida by Rebecca Wright in 2004.

This iridescent silvery fish with the extremely compressed body and very blunt forehead is usually caught at night around lighted docks and bridges in

Lookdown are often spotted at night around piers and bridges in Florida.

southern Florida and the tropics. They're very aggressive and will hit small jigs and metal lures readily. Though small, lookdown are highly regarded as food fish. The closely related Atlantic moonfish *(Selene setapinnas)* has only a moderately steep head profile and short dorsal and anal fin lobes as compared to the extended ones of the lookdown.

ROOSTERFISH *(Nematistius pectoralis)*
Range: Eastern Pacific from Baja California south.
Weight: Average 5-50 pounds. The IGFA record is 114 pounds from La Paz, Baja California, in 1960 by Abe Sackheim.

Roosterfish are probably the most prized inshore species in the tropical eastern Pacific. Author and Capt. Chi-Chi with one plugged off Isla Coiba, Panama, before release.

Roosters are one of the world's great game-fish and also one of the most beautiful. Watching the cocks-comb dorsal fin of the roosterfish coming after a lure or live bait is a special thrill that anglers never tire of. These fish have all the fighting and endurance attributes of the jacks and also frequently provide spectacular leaps when hooked. They can rarely resist live baits, but are a lot fussier about trolled dead baits and frequently follow popping plugs right to boatside before turning off. Though almost always released by sportsmen, they are one of the better eating jacks.

RAINBOW RUNNER *(Elagatis bipinnulata)*

Rainbow runners are common in both Atlantic and Pacific tropical waters. Author took this one at Isla Coiba, Panama.

Range: Offshore waters in both the tropical Atlantic and Pacific oceans.

Weight: Average 3-12 pounds. The IGFA record is 37 9/16 pounds from Isla Clarion, Revillagigedo Islands, Mexico, in 1991 by Tom Pfleger.

This most unlikely-looking member of the jack family is long and slim with distinctive blue and yellow stripes. Some are caught off Florida, but they're more abundant in Bermuda and especially on the Pacific coasts of Panama and Costa Rica, where they're frequently plugged very close to shore.

GIANT TREVALLY *(Caranx ignobilis)*

Range: Tropical Pacific Ocean.

Weight: Average 20-60 pounds. The IGFA record is 160 pounds 7 ounces from Tokara, Kagoshima, Japan in 2006 by Keiki Hamasaki.

This is by far the largest of the slab-sided jacks. Anyone who has struggled through a seemingly endless fight on light tackle with a crevalle can imagine what it must be like to tangle with a giant trevally weighing 100 pounds on casting tackle. Needless to say, few such specimens are landed or boated though they readily hit plugs. This fish provides Hawaiian anglers with great shorefishing opportunities and is also common at Christmas Island, but not along the Eastern Pacific coast.

BLUEFIN TREVALLY *(Caranx melampygus)*
Range: Tropical Pacific Ocean.
Weight: Average 2-15 pounds. The IGFA record is 26 7/16 pounds from Clipperton Island in 1997 by Tom Taylor.

This colorful jack is abundant in some areas of the eastern tropical Pacific, especially in Panama. Also called cobalt jack, it hits popping plugs readily and is a fine gamefish.

DRUMS *(Sciaenidae)*
This large family of inshore species is characterized by their ability to make noises by the vibration of muscles in the swim bladder. Those without bladders grind their teeth together to make noise. There are more than 200 species throughout the world and almost all favor shallow waters, with some being able to adapt to fresh waters.

RED DRUM *(Sciaenops ocellatus)*
Range: Atlantic coast from New Jersey south and the Gulf of Mexico.
Weight: Average 3-50 pounds. The IGFA record is 94 1/8 pounds taken from the surf at Avon, North Carolina, on November 7, 1984, by the late marine biologist Dave Deuel.

This is the premier gamefish of the family and one that can't be mistaken for any other species, with copper coloration and at least one black spot at the base of the tail. Small red drum are called puppy drum, and in the Gulf all sizes are referred to as redfish. Decades ago the common name was channel bass, though they don't resemble any kind of bass. North Carolina's Outer Banks have long been noted for their big red drum, which are caught primarily with bait (especially mullet) in the surf at night and from charter-boats anchored in the rough inlets at Hatteras and Ocracoke. Some are also baited on the bars and from sedge islands in Pamlico Sound, and there are times both there and in the ocean when schools can be spotted—enabling anglers to cast metal

Red drum grow large in Florida's Banana River, where Capt. Shawn Foster guided the author to this 38-pounder. It carried a tag (note blue stringer in back) and is about to be released.

Black drum grow to more than 100 pounds and are common during the spring spawning season in Delaware Bay.

lures and flies to individual drum. The mouth of Chesapeake Bay and the outer islands of the lower Delmarva Peninsula are also noted for big red drum from both boat and surf, but few are caught north of there, though Barnegat Inlet, New Jersey, was actually a hotspot for those fish during the early 1900s. Puppy drum become more important from South Carolina to Florida, and especially in the Gulf where great numbers are caught in shallow waters by casting small jigs (usually tipped with shrimp) and spoons—or on flies. In Florida Bay they often tail like bonefish in very shallow waters.

Red drum have always been highly regarded as food fish in smaller sizes, but there was little commercial interest in big drum until blackened redfish became the rage in New Orleans and netters practically wiped out the Gulf brood stock before the Gulf Fishery Management Council stepped in to control the fishery. Due to the efforts of sportsmen and the Coastal Conservation Association, redfish were made gamefish in Texas, and that movement is spreading throughout the south. Texas has also led the way in hatchery programs for red drum.

BLACK DRUM *(Pogonias cromis)*
Range: Atlantic coast from Delaware Bay south, plus the Gulf of Mexico.
Weight: Average 5-50 pounds. The IGFA record is 113 1/16 pounds from Lewes, Delaware, in 1975 by Gerald M. Townsend.

Somewhat stockier and much duller in coloration than the red drum, the black drum also doesn't compare in gamefish qualities, though they are tough battlers on appropriate tackle. The most important fisheries for large black drum occur in the spring at the mouth of Chesapeake Bay and in Delaware Bay. Formerly rare north of there, schools of black drum have recently been encountered up to Sandy Hook—and have even been hooked on live menhaden and trolled on bunker spoons. Clams fished on the bottom produce most of the big drum, with night fishing being much more effective in Delaware Bay. Anglers are

Spotted sea trout are a prime inshore game and food fish from North Carolina south and throughout the Gulf of Mexico. Capt. Jeff Pfister of Islamorada with an average-sized sea trout from Florida Bay.

often alerted to the likelihood of a bite, especially on calm nights, by the booming sounds produced by large drum, which are the noisiest of all fish. Like the red drum, blacks have an underslung mouth. However, their mouth is fringed with barbels and the throat is armed with crusher teeth that permit feeding on shellfish. Though not basically fish eaters, black drum will hit slow-moving lures on occasion, and even fly fishermen have had good success with them in the shallow waters of Florida's Banana River, where 30- to 50-pounders have been hooked by anglers sight casting from small boats and canoes. Southern anglers catch fair numbers of small black drum while casting jigs tipped with shrimp for redfish and seatrout. Small blacks are much more colorful, with broad vertical black bars on the sides. Even large blacks are good eating, but the scales are so tough that cleaning is a job for experts.

SPOTTED SEATROUT *(Cynoscion nebulosus)*
Range: Atlantic Coast from Cape May, New Jersey south, plus the Gulf of Mexico.
Weight: Average 1-6 pounds. The IGFA record is 17 7/16 pounds from Fort Pierce, Florida, in 1995 by Craig F. Carson.

Probably the most popular inshore small gamefish in the south, the spotted sea-trout is closely related to the weakfish (covered in the section on cooler water species) and mixes with it throughout much of its range. Though identical in shape, the sea-trout sports numerous black spots on its sides and dorsal and caudal fins. They frequent shallow waters and were very vulnerable to gillnetting before that practice was outlawed in Florida and many other areas, while Texas designated the seatrout a gamefish. Though the species has rebounded under strict regulations, the abundance of "gator trout" over 10 pounds in Florida's Indian River still hasn't returned. Spotted seatrout will hit a wide variety of jigs, spoons, and small plugs. Gulf anglers also catch two similar but even smaller species. Sand seatrout *(Cynoscion arenarius),* also called sand trout and white trout, are important panfish in Texas. Though they rarely weigh much more than a pound, the IGFA record is 6 1/8 pounds from Dauphin Island, Alabama, by Steve V. Scoggin in 1997. Sand trout have no spots, but show dark blotches on the back when viewed from above. The silver seatrout *(Cynoscion nothus)* is even smaller and enters bays only during cool-water months. All seatrout are good-eating fish, though the flesh is somewhat soft and doesn't freeze well.

COBIA *(Rachycentron canadum)*
Range: Almost worldwide in tropical and warm temperate water.
Weight: Average 10-50 pounds. The IGFA record is 135 9/16 pounds from Shark Bay, Western Australia, in 1985.

Cobia are among the finest game and food fish of southern waters. This is an average cobia held by a customer of Capt. Joe Alexander in Key West Harbor.

The sole representative of its family, the cobia is a shark look-alike with a long, broad, depressed head. The upper portion of the body is dark brown, and a black stripe extends from the snout to the base of the tail. Though basically a southern species, large cobia are common in Chesapeake Bay during the summer. Only strays are taken north of there, though I was shocked to catch one well inside Raritan Bay off Staten Island, New York, during the summer of 2000 while weakfishing. Cobia are called ling or lemonfish in the Gulf of Mexico, where they are one of the most popular gamefish. Cobia are most frequently encountered around structure such as buoys, channel markers, bridges, and oil rigs or over shallow wrecks. They're not boat-shy and may even settle under your craft. Though incredibly dumb at times, they can be almost impossible to fool on other occasions. During migrations, cobia tend to swim under large rays and can be sight-cast to with lures or live baits such as pinfish. Eels are the most popular bait in Chesapeake Bay. Anglers must be cautious when gaffing cobia as they frequently go wild and can cause a lot of damage if not immediately dropped into a covered fish box. Cobia are one of the best eating fish in the sea, and catches are now strictly regulated by the councils.

TARPON *(Megalops atlanticus)*

Range: Atlantic coast from Virginia south, plus Caribbean and Gulf of Mexico. A few have escaped from the Panama Canal and survived cooler waters at the Pacific end to form a very small population in some area rivers. Some have also been caught at least as far up toward Costa Rica as Isla Coiba.

Weight: Average 5-100 pounds. The IGFA record is 286 pounds 9 ounces taken in Rubane, Guinea-Bissau in 2003 by Max Domecq.

The silver king is among the greatest of gamefish, providing anglers with a big game experience in shallow waters and on relatively light tackle. Its unique appearance with a huge underslung mouth and giant

Tarpon have all the qualities of great gamefish, but are virtually inedible. Capt. Steve Alexander lifts one in Key West Harbor before release.

silver armor-like scales make it impossible to confuse with any other species. Fortunately, the tarpon's fighting and leaping abilities aren't matched by its food value and there's been no objection to treating it as a gamefish in the United States. Indeed, in Florida it's necessary to purchase a $50 permit (in addition to the standard saltwater license) in order to retain one even for record purposes. This species has the unique ability to roll on the surface and gulp air directly, making it possible for them to live in oxygen-depleted waters. They are even frequently found in brackish and fresh waters. Tarpon are migratory, but in winter are abundant in the U.S. only in the always warm waters at the western end of the Florida Keys, though some tarpon overwinter in warmwater outlets of power plants such as the ones at Fort Lauderdale and Palm Beach. As water temperatures rise they start moving north along both coasts, and by summer are caught throughout the Gulf coast and up to Virginia. Only a few stray north of there, though one well over 100 pounds was caught in the Cape May Rips in 2000.

Tarpon will hit a wide range of baits, both dead and alive, plus lures of all sizes. As a general rule, lures with little action and fished slowly are the best bet. Even 100-pound tarpon often hit pilchards, pinfish, and other small baits, but also go crazy over large mullet. Smaller tarpon tend to live around mangrove islands and bridges or in backwaters, while the largest fish favor areas of strong currents such as inlets and the main flows of bridges. Those encountered swimming over flats become the favorite target of flycasters, but the average angler can also soak a chunk of mullet on the bottom and also hook a silver king.

LADYFISH *(Elops saurus)*

Range: Atlantic and Caribbean tropical inshore waters.
Weight: Average 1-3 pounds. The IGFA record is 8 pounds at Sepatiba Bay, Brazil in 2006 by Ian-Arthur de Sulocki.

This slim silvery leaper is the only close relative of the tarpon in North America. Though small, it's a fine gamefish that spends more time in the air than in the water when hooked. A large percentage throw the hook during those acrobatics, and anglers are often happy about that, as ladyfish have no food value and are very slimy to handle.

BONEFISH *(Albula vulpes)*

Range: Tropical inshore waters almost worldwide.
Weight: Average 3-8 pounds. The IGFA record is 19 pounds from Zululand, South Africa, in 1962.

Sight casting for bonefish is one of the most exciting forms of the sport. In the United States it's basically limited to lower Biscayne Bay and the Florida Keys, but

Bonefish are the most sought-after flats fish. Capt. Gary Ellis about to release one at Key Largo.

there's a world of opportunities in such areas as the Bahamas, most of the Caribbean islands (especially Los Roques off Venezuela), and over to Christmas Island in the middle of the Pacific.

There's a special thrill to stalking a swimming or tailing bonefish by flats skiff or wading in order to place a fly, bonefish jig, or bait just ahead of its path—far enough not to spook the fish but still close enough where it can be found. The success ratio in that exercise is often rather discouraging, but dedicated bonefishermen never tire of the challenge or of the smoking runs that may exceed 100 yards and are standard when a bonefish feeding in only a foot or two of water feels the sting of a hook. Bonefish jigs are generally flattish and weigh only one-eighth to one-quarter ounce. I prefer even smaller jigs on ultralight spinning gear in order to avoid spooking the quarry. Live shrimp are usually the best bait and are delivered on a plain hook tied directly to light mono or a fluorocarbon leader. Dead shrimp and strips of conch will also do in many cases, and anglers on Little Cayman use tiny glass minnows for bait. Though sight casting is preferred, bonefish can be hooked by bottom fishing in channels between flats and on both bait and jigs cast into "muds" kicked up by feeding bones on deeper flats. Though eaten by natives in the Bahamas and Caribbean, bonefish are strictly a gamefish in the United States.

SNOOK *(Centropomus undecimalis)*
Range: Atlantic inshore waters from Florida south, including the Caribbean and Gulf of Mexico.

Weight: Average 3-20 pounds. The IGFA record is 53 5/8 pounds taken at Parismina, Costa Rica, in 1978.

Though there are actually four species of snook in Florida, this is the only one that attains any significant size. Snook have relatively slender, silvery bodies distinguished by a black lateral line. Unlike most species,

Snook have long been protected from commercial fishing in Florida, where they are among the most popular game and food fish. Capt. Mark Nichols makes his D.O.A. lures to appeal to St. Lucie River snook.

they shouldn't be grabbed under the gill cover due to the sharp pre-operculum edge that can slice a hand. These shallow-water fish are strictly adapted to warm temperatures and often suffer massive die-offs during winter cold fronts. They favor mangrove areas and such cover as docks and bridges, but some of the largest are caught by fishing live baits in inlets and passes. Snook feed heavily at night, and casting lures or baits to lighted piers is always a good bet. Snook are one of the finest eating of all fish, but have long been protected as gamefish in Florida. A similar species in the Pacific, the black snook *(Centropomus nigrescens),* frequents rivers and shallow waters from Central America to Ecuador and may grow even larger. The record is 57 3/4 pounds from the other side of Costa Rica at Rio Naranjo near Quepos. I've even caught snook in quantity in the Galapagos Islands.

GREAT BARRACUDA *(Sphyraena barracuda)*
Range: Tropical inshore seas worldwide.
Weight: Average 2-20 pounds. The IGFA record is a tie between an 84 7/8-pounder from Scarborough Shoals, Phillipines, in 1991 and an 85-pounder from Christmas Island in 1992.

Next to sharks, swimmers are most fearful of barracuda, which certainly provide a fearsome sight underwater. However, I've yet to see a cuda that didn't keep its distance or failed to back off if I moved toward it. The very few instances of divers or swimmers being hit by cudas involved flashy objects in dingy water or dragging speared fish alongside. Many more injuries have occured with boated cuda or with the very occasional boarding by a free-jumper. Many anglers hate barracuda, which chop off expensive baits and rigs intended for other species—or cut those fish in half during the fight. Yet, the barracuda is also a fine gamefish when taken on appropriate tackle. That's especially the case in shallow waters with long tube lures that are ripped along the surface and produce explosive strikes. Barracuda move onto Florida Keys flats during the winter and save many a day when bonefish can't be located. Not only are their strikes explosive, but they provide smoking runs and great leaps before tiring quickly. Even during the windiest and coolest winter weather, when everything seems to be turned off, I've usually been able

Author with a 42-pound barracuda that hit a tube lure over a Gulf blue hole off Marathon, Florida. This fish was released.

to troll tubes from small boats along channel edges and dark spots over deeper flats to raise cuda regularly.

Barracuda migrate north during the spring, but not too many are caught north of the Outer Banks. There's no mistaking adult barracuda with their large, line-cutting teeth and black blotches on the silvery lower flanks. There are also three small relatives: the northern sennet *(Sphyraena borealis)* and southern sennet *(Sphyraena picudilla),* which grow to only about 15 inches and are common around docks (even in the Mid-Atlantic during late summer in the case of the northern species), and the yellow-striped guaguanche *(Sphyraena guachancho)* that attains two feet. Many other barracudas are found throughout the world, including several along the eastern Pacific coast that don't carry the stigma of ciguatera poisoning which the great barracuda is noted for in Florida and the Caribbean, where it's a prime predator of the reef fish that carry the toxin. That's unfortunate, because all of the barracudas have firm white meat and are excellent to eat. As a practical matter, small cudas caught on the flats should always be safe to eat, but larger specimens from areas with live reefs aren't worth the risk as there's no way to test for ciguatera in advance.

SNAPPERS *(Lutjanidae)*

This family, with more 250 members, is broadly distributed all over the world in tropical and warm temperate waters, and includes some of the finest eating fish. Characteristics of the family include large mouths with eyes set high on the head; pointed pectoral fins; a distinct lateral line; and large scales. Only the most important of the warmwater snappers will be covered here.

RED SNAPPER *(Lutjanus campechanus)*
Range: Atlantic Ocean from North Carolina south, plus the Caribbean Sea and Gulf of Mexico.
Weight: Average 5-15 pounds. The IGFA record is 50 1/4 pounds from the Gulf of Mexico off Louisiana, in 1996 by Doc Kennedy.

The most important snapper for angling in the Gulf is this delicious deep water fish. It is also of great value to the commercial fleet, which has created a situation that the Gulf Fishery Management Council and NMFS have to deal with on a continuing basis. Complicating the situation is the fact that direct fishing isn't the only problem. Bycatch of juvenile reds in shrimp trawling may be even

Red snappers are found in deep waters of the southern Atlantic, but are most important to anglers in the Gulf of Mexico.

more devastating to the population. Some reds are also caught by party boats fishing deep waters off the Atlantic coast from the Carolinas to Florida, but the big volume is in the Gulf. Casual fishermen often identify other reddish snappers caught in shallower waters as reds, but there's no mistaking this stocky snapper, which not only has red sides but also red fins and eyes. Almost all are caught by bottom fishing with bait, though they'll also respond to jigs worked off bottom.

MUTTON SNAPPER *(Lutjanus analis)*

Range: Florida (both coasts) to the Caribbean Sea.

Weight: Average 3-12 pounds. The IGFA record is 30 1/4 pounds from Dry Tortugas, Florida Keys, in 1998 by Richard Casey.

Muttons are inshore snappers that are often primarily reddish, but generally have other colors mixed in and are distinguished by a black, oval-shaped spot on the upper flank of each side. Muttons are excellent eating fish and also fine sport. In addition to being taken in traditional bottom fishing style, muttons sometimes roam the flats and can be sight-cast to with bait, jigs, or flies.

Mutton snappers aren't as bright red as red snappers, and are found in shallower semitropical waters. The black spot on the back is another identifier.

GREY SNAPPER *(Lutjanus griseus)*

Range: Florida and the Caribbean.

Weight: Average 1-4 pounds. The IGFA record is 17 pounds from Port Canaveral, Florida, in 1992 by Steve Maddox.

Better known as mangrove snapper, this species can often be seen swimming around docks and piers in south Florida. Those grays soon become the smartest of fish, carefully checking over everything that drops into the water before attacking it—and avoiding the juiciest morsels attached to a hook! Fortunately, those living in open waters are much more aggressive and provide most of the snapper catch for bridge, shore, and small boat anglers. The least colorful of the snappers, and also one of the slimmest, the gray develops a broad dark feeding stripe from the snout through the eye when excited.

Gray snappers rarely grow as large as this one held by Capt. Joe Alexander after the author caught it on a Gulf wreck off Key West. Note: Faint feeding strip through eye.

YELLOWTAIL SNAPPER *(Ocyrus chrysurus)*

Range: Florida and the Caribbean.

Weight: Average 1-3 pounds. The IGFA record is 11 pounds at Challenger Bank, Bermuda by William DuVal in 2004.

Despite immense pressure, the most popular snapper of the Florida Keys reefs remains abundant and is often chummed up to be caught by the hundreds. The bright yellow coloration defies confusion with any other species, though the name is a problem for California anglers who fish for a yellowtail, which is a much larger member of the jack family. Yellowtails are fine light-tackle gamefish and excellent eating. Most are caught by chumming along the edge of Keys reefs in about 80 to 100 feet and then free-lining glass minnows or other small baits—or letting them drop slowly to bottom on tiny plain jigs. Presentation is the key to that fishing, and in order to get the bait to the right level the pros often make sand balls with both chum and the bait in the middle before dropping them overboard on slack line and then yanking to expose the bait at the proper depth. Yellowtails can often be brought right to the surface by chumming with oatmeal.

Yellowtail snappers, such as this one caught by Baltimore Orioles great Boog Powell, are abundant on Florida reefs.

CUBERA SNAPPER *(Lutjanus cyanopterus)*

Range: Florida, Gulf of Mexico, and the Caribbean.

Weight: Average 10-50 pounds. The IGFA record is 124 3/4 pounds from Garden Bank, Louisiana in 2007 by Marion Rose.

Cuberas have stocky, copper-colored bodies, and in the Atlantic are almost exclusively night feeders rarely caught by accident. Those few anglers who specialize

in catching them in the Keys fish spiny lobsters on the deeper reefs at night. Cuberas also move into the shallows at night and may be caught on bait or lures fished in Caribbean river mouths.

The Pacific cubera *(Lutjanus novemfasciatus)* of the eastern tropical Pacific looks the same as the Atlantic version, but is a completely different fish. Not only do Pacific cuberas feed during the day, but they are extremely

Cubera snappers live in both the tropical Atlantic and Pacific, and sport copper coloration plus large canine teeth.

aggressive and will hit popping plugs cast in shallow rocky waters (generally less than 30 feet) in broad daylight. In my opinion they are the most exciting fish of all to catch on poppers, as the sight of their two large canine teeth coming after a lure is a heart-stopper. Then that slab-sided warrior (which seems incapable of jumping) may completely clear the surface in order to pounce on the plug—hitting the water as if a garage door fell in! Many of those strikes miss the target, and others result in instant cut-offs as the snapper dives for bottom. Much more productive means of catching 20- to 50-pound Pacific cuberas are available, especially trolling live baits and large plugs along the shorelines and making drops to underwater reefs with large live baits or bloody chunks. Costa Rica and Panama are prime areas for these fish, which are very good eating in all sizes and have none of the ciguatera poisoning problems associated with the Atlantic version. The Pacific record is 78 3/4 pounds from Bahia Pez Vela, Costa Rica, in 1988.

MULLET SNAPPER *(Lutjanus aratus)*

Range: Tropical eastern Pacific.

Weight: Average 3-15 pounds. The IGFA record is 45 3/4 pounds from Cerralvo Is., La Paz, Mexico in 2007 by Rolla Cornell.

This snapper's relatively slim body looks like that of a mullet, but it's found in the same areas as the Pacific cubera and shares a similar lifestyle. It, too, will hit popping plugs, and while not as large as a cubera, will fight very well, though not exhibiting the same tendency to dive for bottom structure and break off. Schools of mullet snappers rise up at times during the winter crab hatch on Panama's Hannibal Bank and turn the water red.

Mullet snappers are slimmer than cuberas and more abundant in the eastern Pacific.

SEA BASS *(Serranidae)*

This large family includes many small bottom dwellers, but also such giants as the goliath grouper and California's giant sea bass. Most Serranids (including all of the groupers and sea bass) are hermaphrodites. Females change to males as they grow older and thus are in contrast to almost all other fish species in which the females grow largest. The tropical family members are groupers, which live around obstructions on the bottom and know exactly where to seek shelter when hooked. Bottom fishing for larger groupers requires stout tackle and instant pressure to pull them away from coral. Once the angler has them coming there should be no problem unless a shark shows up. In deeper waters, groupers often pop to the surface with air in their bladders after being fought halfway up. Though the use of live and dead baits on bottom is standard, groupers can also be jigged. Groupers have rounded or squared-off caudal fins and a lower jaw that protrudes, but identification between species is often difficult due to great variations in color. All are excellent eating, though some are involved in the ciguetara problem—especially yellowfin groupers in the Bahamas.

GOLIATH GROUPER *(Epinephelus itajara)*

Range: Tropical inshore waters.

Weight: Average 10-100 pounds. The IGFA record is 680 pounds from Fernandina Beach, Florida, in 1961 by Lynn Joyner.

Once almost wiped out by divers spearing big defenseless targets that won't move from their lairs, the goliath grouper is now protected in Florida and has returned to abundance so fast that it has become a nuisance in some places. Gulf wrecks in about 60 feet are ideal habitat for goliath grouper, and they virtually own many of them, defying anglers to get a hooked snapper or grouper to the surface before they grab it. It's a game hardly ever won by the fisherman. Even should he manage to avoid being cut off by the goliath grouper, which may weigh a couple of

Goliath Groupers grow to huge sizes despite living in relatively shallow waters.

hundred pounds, the fish will have to be released. Goliath grouper are also found under bridges and docks and even in holes on the flats. Their brown body is covered with spots and blotches, and there are four to five diagonal broad dark brown bands. Small goliath grouper may be encountered in mangrove areas and will readily strike jigs. Goliath grouper were highly esteemed as food fish before being protected in Florida, but there are no such restrictions in other countries.

WARSAW GROUPER *(Epinephelus nigritus)*

Range: Florida and Gulf of Mexico.

Weight: Average 50-100 pounds. The IGFA record is 436 3/4 pounds from the Gulf of Mexico off Destin, Florida, in 1985 by Steve Haeusler.

This species replaces the goliath grouper in the depths and is hooked from deeper water wrecks though relatively few have been caught in recent years. The Warsaw's body is uniformly dark, with no spots.

BROOMTAIL GROUPER *(Mycteroperca xenarcha)*
Range: Tropical eastern Pacific.
Weight: Average 30-60 pounds. The IGFA record is 100 pounds from El Muerto Island, Ecuador, in 1998.

This is the largest grouper of the eastern Pacific, though it doesn't appear to be abundant anywhere. It favors relatively shallow areas and is usually hooked on large dead baits.

LEATHER BASS *(Dermatolepis dermatolepis)*
Range: Eastern tropical Pacific offshore islands.
Weight: Average 5-15 pounds. The IGFA record is 27 1/2 pounds from Isla Clarion, Revillagigedo Islands, Mexico, in 1988 by the author.

This most beautiful of the groupers is a relatively rare fish found around offshore islands. My world record was jigged off Clarion Island, but I've also jigged them at Isla Cano, Costa Rica and in the Galapagos. They feature brown bands running vertically on the sides along with numerous white blotches and yellow fringes on all of the soft-rayed fins. The maximum size is believed to be in the 50-pound area.

Leather bass are found around offshore islands in the eastern Pacific. A Royal Polaris mate holds the author's 27 1/2-pound world record from Clarion Island, Mexico.

NASSAU GROUPER *(Epinephelus striatus)*
Range: Atlantic and Caribbean tropical inshore waters.
Weight: Average 3-10 pounds. The IGFA record is 38 1/2 pounds from Bimini, Bahamas, in 1994 by Lewis Goodman.

This is another species protected in Florida where it isn't caught frequently any longer. Not surprisingly, given

Nassau groupers have been protected in Florida for some time, but remain fair game in the Bahamas. There are many color phases, but the black saddle patch at the base of the tail is a sure identifier.

its name, the Nassau is more abundant in the Bahamas. It's a colorful fish with a large saddle-like blotch between the soft dorsal and caudal fins that's a sure identification. A shallow-water fish, it's usually encountered on reefs and around coral heads and will readily strike a variety of live and dead baits plus jigs.

YELLOWFIN GROUPER *(Mycteroperca venenosa)*

Range: Southern Atlantic coast, Gulf of Mexico, and Caribbean.

Weight: Average 5-15 pounds. The IGFA record is 42 pounds from Cypremort Point, Louisiana in 2002 by Jim Becquet.

The outer third of the pectoral fin is a bright yellow or orange and the identifying mark for this grouper, which has many color phases. In addition, dark-brown blotches arranged in rows along the sides and numerous small dark reddish spots are found on this aggressive predator, which hits jigs as well as bait on the reef and is frequently caught while trolling baits or plugs in reef channels and around coral heads.

Yellowfin groupers, such as this one caught by George Poveromo, are common in the Bahamas but often associated with ciguatera poisoning.

BLACK GROUPER *(Mycteroperca bonaci)*

Range: Southern Atlantic coast, Gulf of Mexico, and Caribbean.

Weight: Average 5-50 pounds. The IGFA record is 124 pounds in the Gulf of Mexico off Texas by Tim Oestreich II in 2003.

One of the largest inshore groupers, the black is most abundant in the Atlantic. It's a real tackle-buster due both to its size and propensity for diving into coral bottom. Most pros fish for them with heavy tackle and live baits, such as grunts, held just off bottom. Some blacks are lost even with 6/0 and 9/0 outfits that have drags screwed down. The dark body color is combined with a broad, dark outer zone on the soft dorsal, anal and caudal fins set off by a white margin. Blacks are very active and don't hesitate to hit lures and baits trolled over the reef.

Black groupers are kings of the reef in the Florida Keys. Capt. Joe Alexander with a typical black at Key West.

GAG GROUPER *(Mycteroperca microlepis)*

Range: Atlantic coast from North Carolina south and Gulf of Mexico.

Weight: Average 5-20 pounds. The IGFA record is 80 3/8 pounds from the Gulf off Destin, Florida, in 1993 by Bill Smith.

This species is often confused with the black, which it pretty much displaces in the Gulf. It can be separated from the black by its pale body, indistinct dark blotches, and the whitish edges of the caudal, dorsal, and anal fins plus the first ray of the ventral fins.

Gag groupers are the dominant large grouper in the Gulf of Mexico. Russ Wilson caught this one on a Gulf wreck out of Key West.

RED GROUPER *(Epinephelus morio)*

Range: Southern Atlantic coast, Gulf of Mexico, and Caribbean.

Weight: Average 2-12 pounds. The IGFA record is 42 1/4 pounds from St. Augustine, Florida, in 1997 by Del Wiseman, Jr.

In addition to the highly variable red coloration, this species features green eyes and an elevated second dorsal spine. It's an abundant inshore species that is popular with anglers off the Florida's Gulf coast. Jigs work well, though bait is most commonly used.

Red groupers are abundant both in Florida and the Bahamas.

SCAMP *(Mycteroperca phenax)*

Range: Florida and Gulf of Mexico.

Weight: Average 2-4 pounds. The IGFA record is 29 5/8 pounds at Dauphin Island, Alabama in 2000 by Robert Conklin.

Though one of the smallest groupers, many feel it's the best eating of the family. It features numerous small brown spots on both body and fins.

Scamp aren't abundant and don't grow very large, but many consider them the best eating grouper.

Red hind are small, colorful, and extremely abundant in the Bahamas.

RED HIND *(Epinephelus guttatus)*

Range: Tropical inshore waters.

Weight: Average 1/2 to 2 pounds. The IGFA record is 8 pounds 7 ounces from East Flower Bank in the Gulf of Mexico off Florida in 2004 by Marcus Trapp.

Usually referred to as strawberry grouper due to the large red spots on its body, these small fish aren't abundant on Florida reefs but dominate reefs in the Bahamas, where in some areas it's hard to get a bait or jig through the red hind. The similar rock hind *(Epinephelus adscensionis)* has more coloration over orange-brown spots and a distinctive saddle-like black blotch between the dorsal and anal fins. It's found more on Gulf of Mexico snapper banks, but the record of nine pounds comes from Ascension Island in the South Atlantic.

SHEEPSHEAD *(Archosargus probatocephalus)*

Range: Atlantic coast from Virginia south and Gulf of Mexico.

Weight: Average 1-5 pounds. The IGFA record is 21 1/4 pounds from Bayou St. John, New Orleans, Louisiana, in 1982 by Wayne Desselle. A North Carolina and IGFA Junior record was established in 1999 when Chris Robbins (12) caught a 19 1/4-pounder at the Bonner Bridge over Oregon Inlet.

The largest of the porgy family is distinctive with broad bands of black and silver

Sheepshead feed on crustaceans and require some expertise to hook.

on its compressed sides and a small mouth with protruding flat teeth used to crush shellfish. Though rarely caught north of Virginia, it was once abundant enough in New York that the famed party boat port in Brooklyn was named Sheepshead Bay. They're most abundant in Florida and are a popular panfish caught on shrimp and fiddler crabs from bridges, piers, jetties, and oyster bars. Hooking them requires some expertise, as they suck in baits and then spit out shells—and hooks. Sheepshead are powerful fighters and will also hit jigs, especially when tipped with shrimp.

JOLTHEAD PORGY *(Calamus bajonado)*

Range: North Carolina south, Caribbean, and Gulf of Mexico.

Weight: Average 1-6 pounds. The IGFA record is 23 1/4 pounds from Madeira Beach, Florida, in 1990 by Harm M. Wilder.

The largest of the offshore porgies is basically silver in coloration with brown blotches on the body and a blue line running through the eye. It's the usual porgy caught by southern Florida party boats while bottom fishing in such areas as the Dry Tortugas. The similar red porgy *(Pagrus pagrus)* is an important catch for party boats out of the Carolinas fishing the edge of the continental shelf. It's usually referred to as silver snapper and the record is a 17-pounder from Gibralter. Red porgies are distinguished by having a rounded posterior nostril while all other American porgies have slit-like posterior nostrils.

Southern offshore porgies are much larger than northern species. This one was caught in the Dry Tortugas.

HOGFISH *(Lachnolaimus maximus)*
Range: Atlantic from North Carolina south.
Weight: Average 3-6 pounds. The IGFA record is 21 3/8 pounds at Frying Pan Tower, North Carolina in 2005 by Derek Williams.

The most important tropical member of the wrasse family is considered to be among the best eating of all fish though it's also a ciguatera carrier in the Bahamas where it's most abundant. Divers spear these colorful fish regularly, but anglers struggle to catch an occasional one. Also referred to as hog snapper, the hogfish is red-orange with a pointed steep snout, thick lips, and protruding canine teeth. The first three to four dorsal spines are extended into filaments. A black spot is present on the back at the aft end of the dorsal fin.

Hogfish are not willing biters, though divers spear many of these delicious tropical fish. Pete Barrett caught this one on a Gulf wreck off Key West.

QUEEN TRIGGERFISH *(Balistes vetula)*
Range: Tropical inshore waters.
Weight: Average 1-3 pounds. Up to six pounds or more. The IGFA record is 14 pounds 3 ounces by Martin Gnad at Cancun, Mexico in 2009.

If Pablo Picasso could have designed a fish, this might have been the result. All of the roundish, slab-sided triggerfish are unusual in that the long first spine of the

Queen triggerfish look as though they were designed by Picasso. They're abundant on Bahamas reefs.

dorsal fin is locked into place by the shorter second spine, but can be lowered by depressing the even shorter third spine—or trigger. Triggerfish are good eating, though the leathery skin is tough on knives. Whereas most triggerfish are drab, the queen sports orange and blue colors plus two curved blue bands on the head—and also has filaments that extend from the soft dorsal and caudal fins. Though not common in Florida, queen triggers are abundant in the Bahamas where they hit jigs readily, though it's hard to hook them in their small tough mouth. Larger but far less colorful is the ocean triggerfish *(Canthidermis sufflamen)*, which is often spotted around objects floating in offshore tropical waters and is bold enough to nip at live balao being trolled for sailfish. The equally bland gray triggerfish *(Balistes caprisus)* ranges from the Gulf of Mexico all the way up to Long Island in late summer, where it's commonly caught by bottom fishermen. The record is 13 9/16 pounds from Murrells Inlet, South Carolina, in 1989 by Jim Hilton.

GAFFTOPSAIL CATFISH *(Bagre marinus)*

Range: Atlantic from North Carolina south, plus Gulf of Mexico.

Weight: Average 1-3 pounds. The IGFA record is 10 pounds from Boca Raton, Florida in 2007 by Nicholas Grecco.

Sea catfish have typical slimy catfish bodies with sharp serrated spines on the dorsal and pectoral fins that can inflict painful wounds. Additionally, the gafftopsail features elongated first rays of those fins plus two long barbels on the lower jaw. The blueish gafftopsail is a gamefish that hits a wide variety of lures and is good eating, but most anglers catching them in southern rivers, bays, and surf don't want any more part of them than they do of the lowly hardhead (sea) catfish *(Arius felis)*, which is greenish, has four barbells, and isn't much of a

Gafftopsail catfish are good fighters and decent eating, but anglers such as Mike Ristori would rather not handle their slimy bodies and sharp fins.

fighter. Though usually a pound or less, the sea cat record is a 3 5/16-pounder from Mays Marina, Sebastian, Florida, by Amanda Steed.

BERMUDA CHUB *(Kyphosus sectatrix)*

Range: Tropical inshore waters.

Weight: Average 1-3 pounds. The IGFA record is 13 1/4 pounds from Fort Pierce Inlet, Florida, in 1997 by Sam Baum.

This schooling sea chub with an ovate, somewhat compressed body is a tough fighter on light tackle. Though basically gray, it has two yellow bands on the head and lengthwise brassy bands along the body. They can often be chummed to the boat in big schools on the reefs, but very small hooks are needed to get in their tiny mouths. Bermuda chub are good eating fish.

Bermuda chub are often attracted to chum bags on Florida reefs, but will only hit tiny baits. Jiggs Silber with one from Islamorada.

TRIPLETAIL *(Labotes surinamensis)*

Range: Tropical inshore waters.

Weight: Average 2-10 pounds. The IGFA record is 42 5/16 pounds from Zululand, South Africa, in 1989.

This unusual fish is often spotted laying on its side near channel markers and crab pot buoys where it looks more like a large fallen leaf. The rounded second dorsal and anal fins extend backward toward the caudal peduncal making it appear as if the fish has three tails. Actually they're fine gamefish which hit a variety of lures but especially jigs. Tripletail are good eating and many anglers specialize in seeking them both inshore and along both coasts of central Florida.

Tripletails only require a quick glance to identify. Rick Methot holds one at Islamorada.

WHITE GRUNT *(Haemulon plumieri)*

Range: Tropical inshore waters.

Weight: Average 1/2-2 pounds. The IGFA record is 6 1/2 pounds from North Brunswick, Georgia, in 1989 by J. D. Barnes Jr.

The grunt family, so-named because they produce sounds by grinding their pharyngeal teeth together, includes many small species which are of interest as both panfish and live baits for larger species. The white grunt is the largest and helps fill the bags of bottom fishermen

White grunts are among the most common inshore bottomfish in Florida.

throughout the tropics. Like most other grunts, the interior of the mouth is red. The two largest grunts don't even look like the many smaller and colorful species. The white margate *(haemulon album)* has a grayish body with three black stripes in adults. The record is 15 3/4 pounds from Ambergris Cay, Belize, in 1996 by Carol Barrows. The black margate *(Anisotremus surinamensis)* is more roundish and has black coloration on the forward portion of the sides. The record 12 3/4-pounder was caught in Fort Pierce Inlet, Florida, in 1994 by Carol Napierala.

ATLANTIC COOLWATER INSHORE SPECIES

This section covers species caught primarily inshore and on the continental shelf in the cooler waters characterizing the Mid-Atlantic region from Virginia north through New England and the Canadian Maritime provinces. Many species common during the summer in Chesapeake Bay have already been covered in the previous section, while others to be discussed here are also common to the south but more important in the Mid-Atlantic.

STRIPED BASS *(Morone saxatilis)*

Range: Migratory from North Carolina to Maine and the Canadian Maritime Provinces. Non-migratory river populations from North Carolina to Florida and Gulf of Mexico states. Introduced to California and Oregon rivers and coast. Introduced in fresh waters throughout the United States.

Weight: Average 3-20 pounds. The IGFA record has been broken three times since 1981, with the latest being the 81-pound 14-ounce catch in Long Island Sound off Westport, Connecticut by Greg Myerson on Aug. 2, 2011 while drifting a live eel at night.

The most popular inshore gamefish of the Mid-Atlantic and Northeast is now found all around the country as it thrives in fresh waters as well as salt, even if reproduction isn't possible in most places it's been introduced. Stripers are anadromous fish that require rivers long enough and with sufficient current to suspend their eggs until they're ready to hatch. Only a few along the migratory route meet that requirement, with several in Chesapeake Bay (where they're called rock or rockfish) providing the lion's share of reproduction, though the Delaware and Hudson rivers have sharply increased productivity in recent years and are now strong components of the migratory stock. North Carolina hosts large quantities of migrating stripers off its coast during the winter, but its Albemarle Sound stock appears to be basically non-migratory, and striped bass in all rivers south of there rarely, if ever, go any farther to sea than the river mouth. South Carolina's Santee River population was landlocked by

Capt. Chris De Stefano stands next to the author's 1022-pound giant bluefin tuna caught on Capt. Bob Pisano's *Runaway* out of Brielle in the Mud Hole. It was New Jersey's first "grander," but that state record was broken by seven pounds exactly a year later—also on Pisano's boat.

Author with a 170-pound yellowfin tuna he caught on a Shimano Stella spinning reel and Lamiglas rod after it hit a Yo-Zuri popper. The author fought it for five and one-half hours on a Pesca Panama boat off Isla Montousa, Panama.

This small bluefin tuna is more colorful than the adult. It's about to be released with a NOAA tag. One such bluefin tagged by the author in the Mud Hole off New Jersey was caught the next year in the Bay of Biscay, Spain.

The author in Montauk Harbor with a good-sized mako shark aboard.

Capt. Joe Alexander with a mutton snapper at Key West. Note identifying spot on the back.

Sandbar shark, known as brown shark in New Jersey and New York, with a NOAA tag placed in it by the author.

The author fighting a shark in the Gulf of Mexico.

Billfish are dangerous when they jump at boatside.

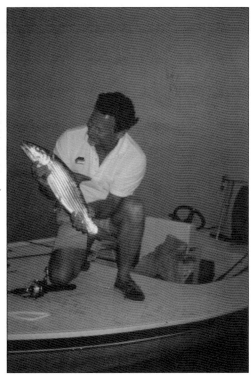

The author with an evening bonefish, before release, caught wading a Keys flat from Richard Stanczyk's skiff out of Bud'N Mary's Marina in Islamorada, Florida.

The author with a Nassau grouper from Walkers Cay, Bahamas. They're now a protected species in Florida—but still fair game in the Bahamas.

Todd Correll with scup (porgy) at Montauk, New York.

The author admires his Goliath grouper before release in the Florida Keys out of Bud N'Mary's Marina, Islamorada. Though once again abundant after being depleted by commercial spear fishing, the species (formerly known as jewfish), is still protected. Florida now prohibits even taking them out of the water before release.

Wahoo trolled off Christmas Island.

dam construction during World War II, but prospered to such an extent that the Santee-Cooper Reservoir system not only provides fine striper fishing but also fingerlings that have been stocked in fresh waters throughout the country.

Stripers can't be mistaken for any other species with their seven to eight black stripes along the sides. The base color can vary from greenish in rivers to the purplish sheen on the back that characterizes migrating bass that have been living in the ocean. Stripers have long been considered a cyclical species, but that may have been the result of overexploitation. As a long-lived species with a high reproductive rate in a variety of waters, there's little likelihood of constant spawning failure. When overfishing destroyed the huge stocks of the 1960s and 1970s, the Atlantic States Marine Fisheries Commission (ASMFC), with backing from the federal government, placed severe restrictions on the fishery and brought it back from low points in the 1980s to a booming fishery once again—but this time with both commercial quotas and recreational catches limited to a bass or two. The largest year classes ever recorded were produced during the 1990s, and exploitation of them is being controlled. Angling release rates soared to over 90 percent, and with that "recycling" of the population there's now no reason to suspect that the migratory stock will ever become scarce again.

Striped bass are the ideal fish for this age, as they thrive in even the worst of waters and are so widely dispersed that everyone gets a shot at them from both shore and boat. Just about any bait will work at times, with seaworms, clams, menhaden (bunkers), and live eels, herring, alewives, mackerel, and anchovies (on the West coast and in Lake Mead) being among the favorites. Lures run the gamut from jigs of all kinds to large plugs. Chumming, chunking, bottom fishing, trolling, jigging, casting, and just about any other technique you can think of all work at times. It's just a matter of conditions and the sizes being sought. That range in size is one of the great attractions of striper fishing, as anglers can have great sport with small bass on light tackle or fish for bass approaching the 50-pound mark on heavy tackle.

Striped bass grow even larger than this world record 76-pounder, which Capt. Bob Rocchetta caught on a live eel off Montauk Point during the eclipse of the moon in July, 1981—only to have the record beaten the next year.

75

BLUEFISH *(Pomatomus salatrix)*

Range: Worldwide in temperate and tropical inshore waters, with the notable exception of the eastern Pacific.

Weight: Average 1-15 pounds. The IGFA record is 31 3/4 pounds taken on Jan. 30, 1972 in Hatteras Inlet, North Carolina, by James M. Hussey.

Bluefish are the sole member of their family, which is widely distributed throughout the world. Its most prominent feature is the jaw armed with small, but sharp, teeth that cut through mono and braided lines with the greatest of ease and serve on a daily basis to chop smaller fish into easily swallowed pieces. They also slice through the fingers of careless anglers, though rarely does a fisherman make that mistake twice! This relatively bland-looking fish has a greenish-blue back blending to a silvery-blue and then a white belly. It lives 10 to 15 years and has a fearsome reputation for slaughtering baitfish, though tank tests at Sandy Hook Marine Laboratory in New Jersey proved they normally stop killing and swim with their prey once satiated. Yet, even those full bluefish could be tempted to feed again by the introduction of different prey, such as an eel.

By far the most important run of bluefish throughout the world occurs along the Atlantic coast, particularly in the Mid-Atlantic and Northeast. During the 1970s and 1980s these fish were so abundant that the weight caught in the recreational fishery far outstripped that of any other marine species in the United States. Long considered to be a cyclical species, adult bluefish were, indeed, very scarce when I was growing up on Long Island—despite the fact that the major object of our dockside fishing with

cane poles during August and September were snapper blues young-of-the-year which always seemed to be abundant despite the seeming lack of spawning-size blues. It wasn't until the latter half of the 1950s that bluefishing started to build up, with the average adult being a pound or two larger each year until it reached a peak when the world record was boated in 1972 and jumbos in the 20- to 25-pound class were not unheard of. There was a theory about a seven-year bluefish cycle at the time, but the

Bluefish are among the most popular fish along the Atlantic coast, and Cyndi Ristori obviously agrees after weighing her jumbo.

blues just kept coming year-after-year. That steady growth in size leveled off and legitimate 20-pounders became unusual toward the end of the century. The volume of bluefish catches also fell sharply, and fringe areas to the north and south experienced bluefish scarcities, but the "cycle" certainly didn't end as catches have continued to remain high in the New York Bight area, which has traditionally supported the most intense fishery for the species.

While recreational landings are way down, the conservation ethic has spread to bluefishing and anglers are now releasing more than 50 percent of the catch rather than keeping a lot of fish which don't freeze well. Its oily flesh, which becomes very strong when not cooked shortly after capture, saved the bluefish from commercial decimation as the fresh fish market can only accept a certain amount each day before the price drops so low as to not cover the cost of shipping. Attempts to freeze and ship bluefish overseas never worked out, and the Bluefish Fishery Management Plan now effectively precludes the development of a new large-scale commercial fishery (such as with purse seines and pair trawlers) even if such an export market were to be developed.

Bluefish are often avoided by anglers seeking striped bass, weakfish, and other game and food fish as they not only interfere with those efforts but also cut off both rigs and sometimes even the quarry! Yet, blues are actually one of the world's great gamefish as they are strong fighters, hit artificial lures, and jump. When they were scarce, blues were also considered a great prize. It's only their abundance and willingness to hit almost anything most of the time, plus the resurgence of previously scarce striped bass that has reduced their standing with many anglers. Bluefishing of the type anglers have been enjoying for four decades in the New York Bight is not only by far the finest for the species throughout the world but also surpasses just about any other small game fishery across the globe—and it occurs literally at the fingertips of one of the world's most densely populated areas.

There seem to be two basic migratory populations along the Atlantic coast. The major run starts from North Carolina and extends north, with blues moving both along the coast and in from distant areas of the continental shelf right behind the mackerel schools, which flee the ravenous choppers by continuing north and east to colder waters. Southern blues move north along the Florida coast during early spring and work up toward North Carolina, though that population is tiny when compared with the northern run. There's also a Gulf of Mexico population that usually consists of small blues but periodically explodes with much larger fish. The most ravenous blues I've ever encountered were at an oil rig off Louisiana where schools of two-pounders attacked hooked Spanish mackerel and literally tore every shred of flesh from their bones. Bluefish attacks I've experienced on the East coast involved a single blue either swallowing a small fish or chopping a larger one and then leaving.

Upon arriving in 50°F waters during the spring migration, bluefish tend to stay near the surface to take advantage of thermal warming and may even be spotted finning. Anglers do best by casting small swimming plugs to them or by trolling on the surface. As waters warm, blues start feeding at all levels and trolling deeper with wire line or downriggers and umbrella rigs or a wide variety of single lures works well, as does the most popular technique in the New York Bight—chumming with ground-up menhaden (bunker) and dropping baits (bunker backs, butterfish, spearing, and so on) back in the resulting slick. When blues are actively feeding, there's great sport to be enjoyed by chasing them and casting popping plugs or dropping diamond jigs to the schools, which are always much thicker than what's observed on the surface.

Surfcasters also get in on this action at times, as do shore fishermen at inlet jetties, river and bay docks, and so on. It's often an all-or-nothing proposition with lures, but there's not much in fishing more exciting than a blitz of jumbo blues in the surf. Soaking bait (such as finger mullet or cut bunker, mackerel or mullet) from the beach often produces blues even when they're not actively feeding.

WEAKFISH *(Cynoscion regalis)*
Range: Atlantic from Cape Cod to Florida and into western Gulf inshore areas.
Weight: Average 1-6 pounds. The IGFA record is 19 3/4 pounds by Dave Alu on menhaden during the night of May 7, 2008 from shore on Staten Island, New York.

Along with striped bass and bluefish, weakfish complete the "big three" of Mid-Atlantic inshore gamefish. All will hit lures readily under most circumstances and are excellent fish to catch on light tackle. Most of the drum family are primarily southern species and were covered in the previous section. Though all have ranges that extend to the south, a few are much more important to the north, and that certainly applies to the weakfish, which is almost an afterthought south of North Carolina where anglers target the similar spotted seatrout. Weakfish aren't abundant in southern areas and rarely attain the sizes achieved by migratory weaks in the Mid-Atlantic. This species has been the most cyclical of all, going from periods of incredible abundance to such scarcity that a coastwise contest during the 1960s had to drop them for lack of entries making a mere three-pound minimum. Yet, during the 1970s weakfish rebounded to such an extent that 10-pounders were common again by the end of the decade. Unfortunately, the same greed and commercial overfishing that devastated

Weakfish have been cyclical, but management could make big weaks such as this one caught by the author in Peconic Bay, Long Island common every year.

the fishery during other periods of the past century prevailed once again before the Atlantic States Marine Fisheries Commission stepped in to manage a fishery which really shouldn't be cyclical since weakfish mature in a year and are long-lived. That fishery built up steadily at the turn of the century and became very good once again. Yet, despite management efforts, weakfish declined to practically nothing by 2011, even though the ASMFC claimed natural mortality was the cause rather than overfishing.

During cycles when they are increasing, large spawning weakfish provide exciting spring runs in Cheasapeake, Delaware, Raritan, Great South, and Peconic bays. They also enter Rhode Island's Narragansett Bay, where they are known by the native Indian name of *squeteague*. Weakfish become steadily larger each year during cycles until 10-to-12-pound "tiderunners" become common before the next crash.

Weaks aren't fighters in the same class as stripers and blues, but their name refers to the fragile nature of their mouth, from which hooks are easily torn. Light tackle is appropriate for these fish, which are usually caught in relatively shallow inshore waters and exhibit no tendency to dive for structure in any case. They may be taken on a wide variety of lures and baits. Jigs are most popular, and should be worked slowly on bottom. In most cases, jigs are tipped with plastic worms, pork rind, squid strips, shedder crab, and the like to provide a larger target or some smell. Small swimming plugs are good bets in the surf, and should also be retrieved very slowly, as weaks seem to shy from fast-moving or highly active plugs and rarely hit poppers. Favorite baits vary widely with areas. For instance, squid is popular to the north, sandworms are number one in Raritan Bay, and shedder crab is favored in Chesapeake Bay. Delaware Bay anglers use shedders, but have also had great success with strips of chicken breast. Since even small weaks tend to swallow baits in a gulp, many small ones are lost due to bleeding. I've found circle hooks to be far superior than others for these fish, as almost all end up hooked in the jaw and can be released without damage. Weakfish are good-eating fish, but the meat is rather soft and must be kept cold. It also doesn't freeze very well.

ATLANTIC CROAKER *(Micropogonias undulatus)*

Range: Atlantic from New York to Florida, Gulf of Mexico.

Weight: Average 1/2 to 2 pounds. The IGFA record is 8 pounds 11 ounces at Chesapeake Bay, Virginia in 2007 by Norman Jenkins.

This is another very cyclical member of the drum family, which is most important in the Mid-Atlantic, particularly in Chesapeake and Delaware bays. Like the weakfish, it made a big comeback during the late 1990s, and by the turn of the century had become a common late-summer catch as far north as Manasquan Inlet, New Jersey, before declining once again. Large schools make booming noises from evening well into the night.

Croakers are a staple fish in Chesapeake Bay, and were on an upswing at the turn of the century. Capt. Mark Nichols jigged this one on his D.O.A. Terroreyz in Florida's St. Lucie River.

SPOT *(Leiostomus xanthuras)*

Range: Atlantic coast from Cape Cod to Florida, plus Gulf of Mexico.

Weight: Average 1/4 to 1/2 pound. Rarely exceeds 1 pound. The IGFA record is 1 pound 7 ounces by Lorraine Gousse at Hampton Roads Bridge-Tunnel, Virginia in 2004.

The smallest fish covered in this book very rarely weighs as much as a pound, but is a most important panfish in the Chesapeake and also makes great live bait in smaller sizes for large weakfish. The distinct brownish spot on the shoulder is a sure identification of this small member of the drum family. It also has 12 to 15 yellowish bars on the sides. Though only occasionally caught as far north as New York City, they are called Lafayettes there, since spot were plentiful during the year that the French hero of the American Revolution arrived.

Spot rarely exceed a pound, but are important panfish in Chesapeake Bay.

NORTHERN KINGFISH *(Menticirrhus saxatilis)*

Range: Cape Cod to Florida.

Weight: Average 1/2-1 pound. The IGFA record is 2 pounds 7 ounces caught by William Graham at Salvo, North Carolina in 2000, but that is well below the maximum size, which is probably closer to 4 pounds. I caught a 2 3/4-pounder in Noyac Bay, Long Island, during 1952—long before the IGFA kept records for such fish.

This beautiful little fish doesn't resemble other members of the drum family and even lacks a swim bladder with which to make noises. It's largely replaced to the south by the very similar southern and gulf kingfishes, but some are caught even in the Gulf of Mexico. All of those kingfish have a short barbel on the chin, and a rounded snout with a tiny mouth. The northern sports an extended second dorsal fin and its seven to eight dusky bands on the sides are darker than those of the southern king while a diagonal bar on the nape forms a V-shaped mark with the first diagonal bar to provide sure identification of the northern species.

Northern kingfish have beautiful distinctive patterns.

This fish and its cousins masquerade under many regional names to the south, including roundhead, sea mink, sea mullet, and whiting. That's probably an effort to separate their real name from the common one for the king mackerel.

Kingfish are shallow-water fish which are most common in bays and the surf. Despite their tiny mouths and lack of size, they hit small baits (seaworms, squid, shrimp, sand fleas) fiercely and are strong fighters. They're also among the best-eating panfish. The southern kingfish *(Menticirrhus americanus)* record is 2 5/16 pounds from Rodanthe, North Carolina, in 1999 by Michael Graham, while the gulf kingfish *(Menticirrhus littoralis)* mark of three pounds ironically also comes from North Carolina. It was taken at Salvo in 1999 by Betty Dike.

COD *(Gadidae)*

This most important food fish family includes prime recreational species in New England. All members of the family have elongated bodies and spineless fins with the ventral fins being located far forward, usually ahead of the pectorals.

ATLANTIC COD *(Gadus morhua)*

Range: Both sides of the North Atlantic and south to Virginia.

Weight: Average 3-30 pounds. The IGFA record is 98 3/4 pounds from Isle of Shoals, New Hampshire, in 1969 by Ambrose Bielevich.

The giant of its family has been recorded far larger than the angling record. A 211 1/2-pounder over six feet long was taken in a trawl off northern

Atlantic cod are favorites of New England anglers as well as winter fishermen in New York and New Jersey.

Massachusetts during May 1895. Other cod from 100 to 175 pounds were recorded during the 1800s, but fishing pressure since then seems to have eliminated such super-sized cod. As with striped bass, anglers seek a 50-pound cod as a real trophy. Easily identified by their three dorsal and two anal fins, cod are usually brownish or greenish in color and have numerous dark spots plus a barbel on the chin. Among the most prolific of fish, a 75-pounder was found to contain 9,100,000 eggs. Yet, massive overfishing by foreign fleets practically destroyed American stocks during the 1960s. After recovering following passage of the U.S. 200-mile fisheries limit, domestic commercial fishermen aided by federal subsidies repeated that devastation within a couple of decades. It wasn't until vast areas of Georges Banks were closed to fishing during the 1990s that cod began returning to abundance around Cape Cod and in Massachusetts Bay. There was an explosion of cod feeding on herring off Block Island that started toward the end of the new century's first decade. Party boats from as far north as Cape Cod ran south to get in on that Bonanza. After a long absence, cod were caught again in decent quantities off the New Jersey coast during the very cold 2011 winter when some cod were even hooked off Ocean City, Maryland.

Cod favor rough bottoms, but can be found even on open bottoms when food is abundant. They are active predators and will eat almost anything from crabs to sand eels, squid, herring, and mackerel. New England anglers do very well jigging cod in deep waters with 8- to 24-ounce diamond and Norwegian metal jigs, but most of the catch further south is taken with clams fished on bottom.

POLLOCK *(Pollachius virens)*

Range: Both sides of the North Atlantic and south to New Jersey.

Weight: Average: 1-30 pounds. The IGFA record is 50 pounds from Salstraumen, Norway, in 1995.

This close cousin of the cod is even more aggressive and likely to rise in the water column. Indeed, they are frequently found feeding well off bottom over deepwater wrecks where they present a prime target for anglers working large metal jigs. The pollock's tail is forked, and it has a distinct and fairly straight white lateral line on a basically bland body. Pollock are prized gamefish, but a step below cod on the plate. While they're also taken on clams, squid is usually a better bait when jigs aren't working. Young pollock, called harbor pollock, are

Pollock are close cousins to the cod and found in many of the same areas, but are more aggressive and tend to swim higher over wrecks.

When it comes to settling the pool on the Viking Starship from Montauk, pollock (left) rarely stand a chance against cod and the huge white hake encountered on deepwater Nantucket wrecks.

very common in schools around northern New England docks and willingly strike small lures. Large pollock are most common over deepwater wrecks even in the Mid-Atlantic, where some of the largest recorded (before recent scarcities due to commercial overfishing) used to come from wrecks 40 to 80 miles offshore in the New York Bight. Though the world record isn't much higher, pollock of 30 to 45 pounds were quite common on those wrecks and even larger wrecks (such as the Andrea Doria) off Nantucket.

HADDOCK *(Melanogrammus aeglefinus)*

Range: Both sides of the North Atlantic and south to New Jersey.

Weight: Average 3-10 pounds. The IGFA record is 14 15/16 pounds from Saltraumen, Germany in 1997.

New Englanders generally rate haddock number one in the cod family for food, and spend a great deal of time trying to catch a relatively small species in preference to the often much larger cod and pollock. Scarcity must make the heart grow fonder, because that wasn't the case earlier last century when haddock were considered poor people's fish. However, that species took the worst beating from foreign ships during the 1960s, and never recovered much before being devastated again by domestic trawlers due to its preference for open bottoms, which provide no hiding places from nets. Yet, conservation measures eventually resulted in a huge haddock comeback. Very similar in shape to the pollock, this bottomfish is instantly identified by the almost straight black lateral line and the prominent black patch over the pectoral fin. Even in the best of times, haddock were never common in the New York Bight, and now they are very rare west of Cape Cod. They hit jigs at times, but most of the catch is taken bottom fishing with baits such as clams, squid, and cut fish on New England banks.

Red hake make up in abundance and good eating what they lack in size and fighting ability.

RED HAKE *(Urophycis chuss)*

Range: Atlantic from Virginia north.

Weight: Average 1-3 pounds. The IGFA record is 12 pounds 13 ounces by Billy Watson from a Mud Hole wreck off New Jersey in 2010.

Formerly known as squirrel hake, this small member of the cod family is of angling importance only in the New York Bight, where it's caught year-round and known as the ling. Ling have soft reddish to brown bodies with an elongated third dorsal fin and very long second dorsal and anal fins, plus a barbel on the chin. Though weak fighters and usually caught from deep waters with tackle that's much too heavy for them, ling are now appreciated as fine food despite the fact that their flesh is soft and must be iced in warm weather. The scarcity of other winter species has made ling an important species in the Metropolitan New York/New Jersey area, where most are caught during winter and summer from 150-to 250-foot-deep wrecks in the Mud Hole. However, there are spring and fall inshore runs when wrecks in 60 feet become populated with ling. Some even move much closer to shore. When the species was more abundant it was even caught in the surf and from piers at night during early winter. Ling are caught by bottom fishing with clams, squid, and cut fish.

WHITE HAKE *(Urophycis tenuis)*

Range: Atlantic south to New Jersey.

Weight: Average 5-30 pounds. The IGFA record is 46 1/4 pounds from Perkins Cove, Ogunquit Cove, Maine, in 1986 by John Audet. This species actually grows considerably larger, as 50- to 60-pounders aren't uncommon.

The white hake looks like a giant red hake with a purplish sheen, and 30- to 60-pounders have huge pot bellies. It frequents deepwater wrecks and is usually the fish spotted in underwater films of the Andrea Doria and other such wrecks. They're not as common in the southern end of their range off New Jersey, but large catches are often made on New England wrecks, especially by boats that fish overnight. White hake appear to be more nocturnal feeders, while cod usually stop biting after dark.

White hake like this 47-pounder boated off a Nantucket wreck by the author have huge bellies and sport a purple sheen.

SILVER HAKE *(Merluccius bilinearis)*

Range: Atlantic from Virginia north.

Weight: Average 1/2-2 pounds. The IGFA record also comes from Perkins Cove, Ogunquit, Maine. It was caught in 1995 by Erik Callahan and weighed 4 1/2 pounds.

Quite unlike the other cod and hake, this fish has a slim, silvery body and a large mouth full of small, sharp teeth. Though of little angling interest elsewhere, in New York Bight it's known as whiting and used to be the most important winter species. Perhaps the most abundant species in the area, it was heavily impacted by foreign trawlers in the Mud Hole during the 1960s, but after coming back was virtually wiped out by local small mesh trawlers who killed baby whiting by the millions in order

Silver hake are known as whiting in New York Bight. There used to be a huge winter fishery for them until small mesh draggers virtually wiped out the most abundant species in the area.

to box a few of marketable size. By 2000 there were so few of these once superabundant fish left that party boat anglers who caught them didn't even know what they were. Much more aggressive than the other hakes, whiting readily hit diamond jigs, though most are caught on strips of squid, mackerel, herring or, best of all, other whiting. When possible, drifting is more effective than anchoring during the day, though whiting hit best at night. That was particularly true during the decades of abundance when whiting were caught in huge numbers after dark from December to February from ocean piers, jetties, and the surf. At times they were so abundant that whiting chasing bait in the surf during frigid winter nights would be thrown up onto the beach by waves and freeze on the spot. Locals walked those beaches to fill sacks with what came to be known as frostfish.

ATLANTIC MACKEREL *(Scomber scombrus)*

Range: Temperate and cold waters of the Atlantic.

Weight: Average 1-21/2 pounds. The IGFA record is a 2 5/8-pounder from Kraakvaag Fjord, Norway, in 1992, but they grow to at least four pounds.

This is one of the most abundant fish in the northern Atlantic, and very important not only as food and bait but

Atlantic mackerel come aboard in multiples as anglers such as Bobby Correll use jigging rigs to catch them during the spring migration from Virginia to New England.

as an important food source for predators ranging from bluefin tuna to striped bass and cod. Anglers enjoy great sport jigging them during the migratory run, which starts off Virginia in March and reaches the New York Bight around mid-April. In addition to their value as fresh food, mackerel are frozen in large quantities for use later as bait for sharks, striped bass, bluefish, and tuna. This is a very important party boat fishery for two to four weeks, and those boats are packed with anglers who use jigging rigs consisting of several small hooks with tubes that are jigged at various depths to catch several mackerel at a time. Even plain hooks will work at times. Rarely is chumming required, as skippers usually read the schools on fishfinders and drop the lures to them. Mackerel schools tend to follow the activity and provide long drifts. By early May, with the water temperature over 50°F and bluefish on their heels, mackerel quickly move east. Some may be encountered at Block Island in June and July, but most summer mackerel fishing occurs north of Cape Cod. They're a very popular inshore catch off New Hampshire, Maine, and the Canadian Maritime provinces during summer, and Massachusetts striper fishermen seek them for prime live bait. The fall run to the south starts late and doesn't attract as much angling interest in the New York Bight during December and January. Though most mackerel are dragged aboard on relatively heavy boat rods several at a time, they're actually fine fighting fish when hooked individually on ultralight tackle.

WINTER FLOUNDER (*Pseudopleuronectes americanus*)
Range: Atlantic south to Delaware.
Weight: Average 1/2-2 pounds. The IGFA record is 7 pounds from Fire Island, New York, in 1986 by Einar Grell.

This small flounder is highly prized as both a food and sport fish from central New Jersey north. It comes in from the sea during fall to overwinter in bays before spawning during early spring and returning to sea. The heavy fishery from New Jersey to Cape Cod occurs during the spring before other inshore fisheries get started. This right-eyed flounder has a tiny mouth and varies greatly in color. Few caught in coastal

bays and rivers exceed three pounds, but "snowshoes" (which often develop some yellowish coloration on the white side) of three to five pounds or more are caught each spring in such areas as Gardiners Bay, Long Island, and at the Hooter Buoy off Block Island. Flounders are very

Winter flounder are usually only a pound or so, but those weighing at least three pounds are found in some areas and referred to as snowshoes.

aggressive considering their small size and will suck in seaworms, mussels, and strips of clam in a flash. Chumming with crushed mussels, corn kernels, rice, or a frozen mixture with ground clams is usually a must for large catches. Flounders take a beating from trawlers while at sea during the summer, and the population was depleted at the beginning of this century. There is hope that fisheries management will improve the situation, as (in addition to severe recreational and commercial restrictions) trawling for winter flounder on their summering grounds has been prohibited. A similar, but smaller and thinner offshore flounder, the yellowtail, is rarely hooked by anglers but was of much greater commercial importance before also being netted into relative scarcity.

SUMMER FLOUNDER *(Paralichthys dentatus)*
Range: Cape Cod to South Carolina.
Weight: Average 1-5 pounds. The IGFA record is 22 7/16 pounds from Montauk, Long Island, in 1975 by Capt. Charie Nappi.

This left-eyed flounder is called "fluke" north of southern New Jersey, and simply "flounder" south of there. It's easily distinguished from the winter flounder by its large mouth full of small teeth. Also in complete contrast to its cousin, the fluke winters offshore before moving inshore during spring—and returning offshore in the fall to spawn. Fluke feed primarily on fish, and eagerly pounce on many baits and lures. It is the most popular recreational fish in the Mid-Atlantic, where most are caught from drifting boats both in bays and rivers and along the coast. While the sport catch has traditionally come almost entirely from inshore waters, there has been more fishing for fluke on lumps out to six miles or so offshore in recent years, particularly when sand eels are present to hold them there. Small mesh trawlers netting fluke when they were concentrated during winter on the edge of the continental shelf devastated the stocks during the 1980s by killing the young-of-the-year in addition to marketable fluke. Fishery management since then has brought stocks back by placing quotas on netters while strictly regulating recreational sizes, bag limits, and seasons. Most fluke are caught on live killies or dead baits such as spearing, sand eels, strips of squid, and strips of other fish including fluke. Small live snapper

Summer flounder may grow larger, but this 22 7/16-pound fluke caught by Capt. Charlie Nappi off Montauk Point, Long Island, on a live snapper bluefish in 1976, has remained the IGFA All-Tackle record for one of the most heavily fished species.

Fluke are great sport for kids. Dr. George Gabuzda with his family on the author's boat at Manasquan Ridge.

bluefish are ideal baits during late summer for large fluke; in fact, that was what the 22-pound-plus world record was tempted by in 60-foot depths on mussel bottom just south of Montauk Lighthouse. In contrast to usually plain rigging for flounders, fluke fishermen often employ spinners, bucktails, and other attractors in conjunction with their baits, which are frequently mixed—such as killies and squid. Fluke of 10 pounds or more are called "doormats" and are the fluke fisherman's trophy. Those specializing in catching them tend to use large baits such as long strips of fish, whole squid, and smelts. Though basically associated with sand and mud bottoms, fluke feed everywhere, and the larger ones seem to prefer mussel bottoms and the vicinities of wrecks and other rough bottom.

Fluke are replaced south of North Carolina by the southern flounder *(Paralichthys lethostigma),* which lacks the brown spots on the dark side. The record for that species is 20 9/16 pounds caught from Nassau Sound, Florida, in 1983 by Larenza Mungin. Another flatfish often caught while fluking is the windowpane, a small fish that also has a relatively large mouth and teeth but is so skinny that it's possible to hold it up to the sun and look through the body.

BLACK SEA BASS *(Centropristis striata)*

Range: Cape Cod to Florida and Gulf of Mexico.

Weight: Average 1/2-3 pounds. The IGFA record is 10 1/4 pounds by Allan Paschall off Virginia Beach, Virginia in 2000.

This is the only member of the sea bass family that lives primarily in cool waters, though some are also found in the ocean off Florida and in the Gulf both on the snapper banks and inshore. Like the groupers, sea bass change sexes as they grow, but in their case it's very noticeable, with drab females becoming gaudy males with a beautiful blue-black or indigo coloration, a prominent hump on the head, and white fleshy tabs on the fins. Basically, these fish have movements similar to those of the fluke as they winter on the edge of the continental shelf and move inshore during spring before returning offshore in fall. Sea bass favor wrecks and rough bottoms where they're often caught in large quantities on clams and

All large sea bass are males, distinguished by the hump on the head and white fringes on fins.

88

squid. They're aggressive enough to hit diamond jigs with some frequency. Jumbos of three to seven pounds or more are most frequently caught during the winter and early spring on deepwater wrecks. Sea bass are among the very best of eating fish.

SCUP *(Stenotomus chrysops)*

Range: Cape Cod to North Carolina.

Weight: Average 1/2-3 pounds. The IGFA record is 4 9/16 pounds taken from Nantucket Sound, Massachusetts, in 1992 by Sonny Richards.

Scup are very important inshore bottomfish from Cape Cod to New Jersey. The roundish, silvery fish is called porgy in the Mid-Atlantic and is particularly popular with fishermen who appreciate the eating quality of a fish that is rarely filleted due to its large scales and slim sides. Like the fluke and sea bass, porgies winter offshore and move in during the spring when there's a big fishery in Nantucket Sound. Summer and early fall fishing is good off eastern Long Island plus Long Island and Block Island sounds, but the New York Bight area has been productive in recent years only during the fall and even then the porgies are smaller than those caught to the east. This is another species that was devastated by the small mesh nets offshore as well as even smaller mesh in other fisheries such as squid, which killed tiny porgies by the millions as bycatch. Management finally started bringing this species back by 2000, and recreational regulations have been liberalized. During the 1960s, anglers in the New York Bight were able to fill burlap bags with porgies over a foot long from spring through fall. Small pieces of clam and squid are used for porgies, which have tiny mouths and often peck at baits, though at times they are very aggressive. Porgy pros usually chum with frozen logs on bottom, as they do for flounders.

Scup are better known to Long Island anglers as porgies. These were caught by Dr. Don Proferes and his son Jimmy off Montauk Point.

TAUTOG *(Tautoga onitis)*

Range: Nova Scotia to South Carolina.

Weight: Average 1-8 pounds. The IGFA record is 25 pounds from a wreck off Ocean City, New Jersey, in 1998 by Anthony Monica.

This distinctive species is one of only two cool-water members of the tropical wrasse family. Its cousin, the cunner (bergall, sea perch, chogset, choggie), is a much smaller version with small protruding teeth that frequents the same rough bottoms and is usually regarded as a nuisance. The larger sizes (one to three pounds), encoun-

Tautog are known as blackfish off Barnegat Inlet, New Jersey, where this 12 1/4-pounder was boated.

tered on offshore wrecks or inshore Maine waters, provide excellent-eating fillets, however. The Indian name tautog is commonly used both in New England and from southern New Jersey to Virginia, where they are also common before becoming a rarity in the Carolinas. However, from central New Jersey through Long Island the same fish is invariably called blackfish.

Tautog are quite distinctive, with mottled brown or black bodies, a broad caudal fin, and a white chin on the larger specimens. The lips are thick and the teeth protrude slightly, enabling the fish to pick off shellfish that are sent back to crusher teeth in the throat. Anglers catch tautog by fishing the bottom with green, calico, blueclaw, fiddler, or hermit crabs. There's lots of skill involved, since the nibble indicates the tautog is preparing to suck it in, at which time there's just a moment when the shell is being crushed before being spit out with the hook. Striking at just the right moment when there's a solid feel is the key to success. Soft baits such as clams are best early in the spring before cunners become active. Adult tautog winter offshore and become semi-dormant in the coolest temperatures, but some of the largest are caught during the winter from New Jersey to Virginia. They move into shallow water to spawn during spring and return to deeper areas for summer before heading inshore to feed in fall. Once strictly of interest to sportfishermen, and a consistently abundant species of little commercial value, all that changed during the 1990s as Asian restaurants paid big money for tautog that will live indefinitely in small tanks. Within a few years the population was depleted and management is now in place to prevent further overfishing. Tautog have tough oily skins and defy scaling, but are excellent eating when skinned and filleted.

GREAT NORTHERN TILEFISH *(Lopholatilus chamaeleonticeps)*

Range: Nova Scotia to Florida and eastern Gulf of Mexico.

Weight: Average 10-30 pounds. Grow to about 60 pounds. The IGFA record is 63 1/2 pounds by Dennis Muhlenforth from Lindenkohl Canyon off New Jersey in 2009.

This beautiful deepwater species lives in a very narrow band of water near the edge of the continental shelf and is subject to periodic disappearances. It wasn't even known to scientists until a cod trawler brought 5,000 pounds in from south of Nantucket in May 1879. A fishery quickly developed before a massive die-off occurred in 1882, when tilefish were spotted floating all over the North Atlantic—and not another was caught for ten years. Scientists suspect an invasion of extremely cold water into the 47° to 53°F range which the species prefers caused that disaster. Yet, the population rebounded again and was strong enough to support a party boat sportfishery off New York and New Jersey in the 1960s and 1970s before commercial overfishing reduced the population too much, though that fishery has come back and provides a good alternative for canyon fishermen. Tilefish are colorful, with a yellow-spotted upper body and a bright yellow fleshy tab on the head. They feed on lobsters and crabs, and their flesh has some of that flavor. Anglers usually catch them while drifting on bottom in 450 feet or more with whole squid. The use of wire, Dacron, or strong braided lines is a must in those depths. A sim-

Tilefish used to be abundant along the edge of the continental shelf in 450-foot depths of Long Island. Tilefish catches like this by the author in the early days of the sport fishery are once again possible—though most of the tilefish are now much smaller.

ilar, though duller, species, the blueline tilefish, is more abundant in warmer waters to the south, with a record of 20 1/4 pounds from Norfolk Canyon.

STRIPED SEA ROBIN *(Prionotus evolans)*

Range: Cape Cod to northern Florida.

Weight: Average 1-2 pounds. The IGFA record is 3 3/8 pounds from Mt. Sinai, Long Island, in 1988 by Michael B. Greene Jr.

This is the larger of two sea robins commonly caught by bottom fishermen in the Mid-Atlantic. The smaller northern sea robin is slim with a dull body, while the striped sea robin has two or more dark stripes along the body plus orange shading on the lower body and fin tips. They move inshore during spring and will hit almost any bait and even lures. Sea robins have bony heads covered with sharp projections, broad, wing-like pectoral fins, and three lower, stiff, separate pectoral rays which seem to be used for feeling on the bottom. Between the head and sharp dorsal fins, sea robins require careful handling—but their mouth provides a good gripping point. Most anglers throw them back, but sea robins are actually good to eat, and are considered gourmet food in Europe. They also make excellent strip baits for fluke.

Striped sea robins have impressive "wings" and fight hard, but are regarded as a nuisance by Mid-Atlantic fluke fishermen.

NORTHERN PUFFER *(Sphoeroides maculatus)*

Range: Cape Cod to northern Florida.

Weight: Average 1/2-1 pound. Rarely over two pounds.

This is one of many puffers found around the world, but the only one common in Atlantic temperate waters. That's fortunate, because puffers produce a powerful toxin, tetrodoxin, which is concentrated in their internal organs and skin, but can also be found in the meat of some species. The northern puffer has only very small concentrations in internal organs and the meat is safe to eat when the fish is cleaned by making a cut behind the head and the edible back is pulled away from the rest of the fish. What's left is breaded and fried to become "chicken of the sea." That was a real treat when I was a young-

Puffers are slow but, as Mike Ristori demonstrates, they can blow themselves up with either water or air to discourage predators.

ster and blowfish were the most abundant inshore species on Long Island. During the 1960s they almost disappeared for reasons not clear. I suspect the huge increase in bluefish around the same time may have been responsible, since blues would load their stomachs with tiny puffers. Adult puffers have no such problem since they are able to blow themselves up with either water or air to discourage predators. Puffers have teeth that are fused to form a beak capable of crushing shellfish. They nibble at any bait and are expert bait stealers. Blowfish began a comeback in Barnegat Bay, New Jersey in 2010—and could return to their former abundance. Species caught in the south should be released, since some carry more toxin than the northern species.

PACIFIC TEMPERATE AND COLD WATER SPECIES

CALIFORNIA YELLOWTAIL *(Seriola lalandei)*

Range: Central California to Baja California.

Weight: Average 5-20 pounds. The IGFA records is 109 1/8 pounds by Masakazu Taniwaki from Ohara, Chiba, Japan in 2009.

Yellowtails of the Pacific can't be confused with yellowtail snappers of the Atlantic. They're highly-regarded gamefish found on both sides of the Pacific, though they average almost twice as large in New Zealand, where this was a common size off White Island.

Though this member of the jack family is identical to yellowtails caught on the other side of the Pacific, those caught here average far smaller than their New Zealand counterparts (the record there is 114 5/8 pounds), and the IGFA keeps records for them separately. The California yellowtail looks like a somewhat elongated amberjack with a light lemon-yellow stripe running along the median line into the all-yellow tail. A voracious feeder, it is usually caught on live baits fished around kelp beds off southern California, the Baja California coast, and up into the Sea of Cortez. San Diego long-range party-boats make trips into Mexican waters in order to find prime yellowtail fishing, but there are also many productive California waters. Trolling is effective at times, and yellowtails will hit metal jigs. Unlike many other jacks, the yellowtail is a good eating fish.

PACIFIC BARRACUDA *(Sphyraena argentea)*
Range: Point Conception, California south to Magdalena Bay, Baja California.
Weight: Average 2-5 pounds. The IGFA record is 28 3/8 pounds by Jilberto Cansari at Isla Secas, Panama in 2010.

Though much smaller than the great barracuda of the Atlantic, the California version may be the most popular since it's a willing biter around kelp beds and very good eating without any concern about ciguatera. This surface species is caught primarily on live anchovies or by casting or trolling small lures. It has a brownish body with no blotches.

Pacific barracudas aren't as large but are good eating and have none of the ciguatera poisoning problem associated with the great barracuda in Florida.

WHITE SEABASS *(Atractoscion nobilis)*
Range: San Francisco to Magdalena Bay, Baja California.
Weight: Average 7-15 pounds. The IGFA record is 83 3/4 pounds from San Felipe, Mexico, in 1953 by Lyle Baumgardner.

This west coast giant of the drum family looks like a huge weakfish rather than any sort of bass. It was almost fished out in California but is making a big comeback. A long-lived fish, it was fairly abundant as late as 1949 when 65,500 were caught on party boats and 40-pounders weren't uncommon. Hopefully, white seabass fishing of that quality is down the road. These fish are usually found around kelp beds in 15 to 25 fathoms from May to September and are taken on both live baits such as anchovies, sardines, and Pacific mackerel as well as slowly fished lures. Night fishing with live squid on bottom is effective. Like weakfish, they have good eating but relatively soft flesh that requires icing. Another family member of some importance is the orangemouth corvina *(Cynoscion xanthulus),* which provides action for surfcasters in southern California as well as to anglers probing California's landlocked Salton Sea. The record for that species is 54 3/16 pounds from Sabana Grande, Guayaquil, Ecudaor, in 1992.

GIANT BLACK SEA BASS *(Stereolepis gigas)*
Range: Point Conception, California through Baja California and the Sea of Cortez.
Weight: Average 5-100 pounds. The IGFA record is 563 1/2 pounds caught by James D. McAdam Jr. on Aug. 20, 1968 at Anacapa Island, California.

This relatively rare member of the temperate bass family *Percichthyidae* (related to the striped bass and white perch rather than groupers) was seriously overfished and has been protected by a moratorium in California. These fish are very long-lived, and a 435-pounder was estimated at 72 to 75 years. Just as with goliath groupers in Florida, divers had no trouble eliminating most of these giants from their relatively shallow-water habitats. They mature between 11 and 13 years when they're 50 to 60 pounds, and favor rocky bottoms near kelp beds. Live or dead baits fished off bottom account for most hook-ups.

CALIFORNIA HALIBUT *(Paralichthys californicus)*
Range: Klamath River, California, to Magdelana Bay, Baja California.
Weight: Average 2-10 pounds. The IGFA record is 58 9/16 pounds from Santa Rosa Island, California, in 1999 by Roger Borrell.

The large mouth with numerous sharp teeth plus a high arch in the lateral line above the pectoral fin identify this member of the left-eye flounder clan, which actually ends up being right-eyed 40 percent of the time. These relatively small halibut are sought after on sandy bottoms in less than 10 fathoms and even come into the surf at times. Drifting with live baits and jigging are effective methods for this aggressive game and food fish.

PACIFIC HALIBUT *(Hippoglossus stenolepis)*
Range: Bering Sea to Santa Rosa Island, California.

Weight: Average 10-100 pounds. The IGFA record is 459 pounds from Dutch Harbor, Alaska, in 1996 by Jack Tragis.

Not only is this much larger halibut a right-eyed flounder, but it has a lunate caudal fin as compared to the California halibut's rounded tail. The large halibut's lower jaw also extends to the front edge of the eye as compared to the California's, which extends well beyond the eye. Most of the time there's no need to wonder which species is involved due to size, but there is some overlapping in near-shore areas in northern California. Pacific halibut are common to the north and available in greatest quantities off Alaska, where most are taken in deeper waters. Size varies greatly, and the same area that produces 15- to

Pacific halibut grow to hundreds of pounds, but most of the catch taken at Sitka consists of the sizes displayed by the author and Penn Reels ex-president Herb Henze.

40-pounders one week could give up a 300-pounder the next. The most important strictly saltwater fish of the Pacific Northwest has long been regulated by a treaty between the United States and Canada to prevent overfishing, and regulations are constantly being tightened on sportfishing for halibut due to its increasing popularity. Most halibut are caught by bottom fishing with large fish baits or even salmon guts. Some are also taken with large metal jigs. Depths of 200 to 300 feet are routine and currents constitute a big problem in some areas, but the possibility of catching a 300- to 400-pounder is exciting enough, and it's hard to beat smaller halibut as an eating fish.

DIAMOND TURBOT *(Hypsopetta guttulata)*
Range: Cape Mendocino, California to Cabo San Lucas.
Weight: Average 1/2-1 pound. Up to four pounds.

This small inshore right-eyed flounder is a California favorite easily identified by its diamond shape and green color with pale blue spots. It favors muddy or sandy bottoms in bays and sloughs, and is caught year-round with tiny pieces of clam or shrimp.

STARRY FLOUNDER *(Platichthys stellatus)*
Range: Point Arguello, California to the Aleutian Islands.
Weight: Average 1-3 pounds. No IGFA record, but reputed to attain 20 pounds.

Though in the right-eyed flounder family, this species is more often left-eyed. The most popular inshore flatfish of northern California is abundant from December through March and will hit pieces of sardine, clam, shrimp, squid, and seaworms. The dark-brown body is surrounded by alternating patterns of orange/white and dark bars on the fins. This flounder has been found as far as 75 miles upstream in the Columbia River.

SCORPIONFISH *(Scorpaenidae)*

This family includes about 400 species worldwide, including more than 100 in the rockfish genus Sebastes. The rockfishes are of great importance to bottom fishermen from California to Alaska, but their numbers have been greatly diminished by commercial overfishing. In addition to the three covered here, there are some others of importance. The olive rockfish *(Sebastes serranoides)* frequents California reefs and kelp beds; the greenspotted rockfish *(Sebastes chlorostictus)* is a deepwater species; the copper rockfish *(Sebastes caurinus)* ranges from shallow waters to 100 fathoms all the way from Baja California to the Gulf of Alaska and has a record of 7 1/4 pounds from Drakes Bay, California; the chilipepper *(Sebastes goodei)* ranges from British Columbia to Magdelana Bay and has been caught up to 3 3/8 pounds at San Clemente Island, California; the quillback rockfish *(Sebastes maliger)* favors rocky bottoms in less than 40 fathoms from Kodiak Island to Point Sur, California, and has a record of 7 1/4 pounds from Depoe Bay, Oregon; the bocaccio *(Sebastes paucispinis)* has been caught up to a 26 5/8-pounder at Elfin Cove, Alaska, and is also prized in California; and the colorful tiger rockfish *(Sebastes nigrocinctus),* a solitary species popular in the Pacific Northwest, with the 7-pound record coming from Chugach Island, Alaska.

YELLOWEYE ROCKFISH *(Sebastes ruberrimus)*

Range: Ensanada, Baja California to Prince William Sound, Alaska.

Weight: Average 5-10 pounds. The IGFA record is 39 1/4 pounds by David Mundhenke at Whalers Cove, Alaska in 2000.

The largest and most desired of the rockfish, this brilliant orange/red fish with a bright-yellow eye that usually bulges out after being brought up from the depths is caught primarily in deep waters offshore. A very long-lived species, it's a fine food fish and now protected with quotas and bag limits.

Yelloweye rockfish are the largest of their extensive clan. With brilliant orange coloration, these very long-lived rockfish live in deep water and have been overfished by commercial fishermen.

CANARY ROCKFISH *(Sebastes pinniger)*

Range: Northern Baja California to the Gulf of Alaska.

Weight: Average 1-2 pounds. The IGFA record is 10 pounds from Westport, Washington, in 1986 by Terry Rudnick.

This is the most important commercial rockfish and is found in depths from 50 to 300 feet. It has an orange body with three bright-orange stripes across the head, which also has small spines.

BLUE ROCKFISH *(Sebastes mystinus)*
Range: Northern Baja California to Sitka, Alaska.
Weight: Average 1/2-1 pound. The IGFA record is 8 3/8 pounds from Whaler's Cove, Alaska, in 1994 by Dr. John F. Whitaker.

This small, inshore, schooling rockfish is easily accessible to anglers. It has a bass-like body with generally slate-blue coloration and blotches on both back and sides. Like the similar and slightly larger black rockfish *(Sebastes melanops),* blues will rise to the surface at times while feeding on sand lance. The record for blacks is ten pounds from Puget Sound, Washington, in 1986 by Dr. William J. Harris.

SALMONS

Though generally consigned to books about freshwater fishing, the salmons (except for landlocked species) are actually anadromous fish like the migratory striped bass, living in salt waters and only returning to rivers to spawn. Unlike the striper, which makes the spawning journey year after year, Pacific salmon are semelparous—which means they have a one-way trip to spawn and die. While some anglers envision Pacific salmon fishing as involving casting in rivers to fish that are no longer feeding, most of that sport (except for sockeyes) actually involves bait and lure fishing in the ocean and near rivermouths when the salmon are still putting on poundage to support their last glorious journey and are in prime condition. The most popular bait for salmon is a small herring plug, cut so it spins when retrieved or slow-trolled.

CHINOOK SALMON *(Oncorhynchus tshawytscha)*
Range: Central California to Bering Sea.
Weight: Average 10-30 pounds. The IGFA record is 97 1/4 pounds from the Kenai River, Alaska, in 1985 by Les Anderson, but a 126-pounder was caught commercially near Petersburg, Alaska.

Chinook salmon are one of the major species encountered by anglers from northern California to Alaska. The author's 30-pounder is a fairly common size at Sitka, Alaska.

Chinooks, or kings, are the largest of the salmons and also have the most precise spawning river requirements due to both their size and that of their eggs. While young kings in southerly rivers generally move directly toward estuaries after emerging from the gravel of spawning beds, those in northern Alaska rivers may remain there for a year or two. Kings are identified by the small black spots on tail lobes. They generally spawn at ages four to seven. These are the most desired salmon due to their large size, which varies greatly with various river runs. Kings of 30 to 50 pounds are routine in the famed spring Kenai River run, and many much larger are boated despite heavy angling pressure. While 30-pounders are common in Alaska's ocean fishery, 50-pounders occupy the same status as a trophy size, as is the case with striped bass.

COHO SALMON *(Oncorhynchus kisutch)*

Range: Central California to Chukchi Sea.

Weight: Average 5-10 pounds. The IGFA record is 33 1/4 pounds—a landlocked fish from the Salmon River, New York.

Cohos, or silver salmon, mostly spawn at two or three years and don't grow as large as kings. They are slimmer than kings and have black spots on the upper portion of their body right into the upper tail lobe. These fish do a lot of jumping when hooked, but I personally don't rate them very highly as fighting fish.

Coho or silver salmon such as this one caught by Capt. Tom Ohous from his charter boat at Sitka are primarily caught there from mid- to late-summer.

CHUM SALMON *(Oncorhynchus keta)*

Range: Coastal and inshore waters of the Pacific Northwest.

Weight: Average 5-10 pounds. The IGFA record is 35 pounds from Edye Pass, British Columbia, in 1995 by Todd A. Johansson.

Chum salmon are the third of Alaska's big three salmon species caught in salt water.

Chum, or dog, salmon are the most abundant of the Pacific salmons in biomass but aren't as important to anglers as the king and coho. Though this species has black specks on the back, there are no black spots on the tail. They spawn at ages from three to five, mostly from July to November in Alaska.

PINK SALMON *(Oncorhynchus gorbuscha)*

Range: Coastal and inshore waters of the Pacific Northwest.

Weight: Average 2-5 pounds. The IGFA record is 14 pounds 13 ounces by Alexander Minerich at Monroe, Washington.

Pinks are also called humpbacks or humpys because the male changes from a slim fish to one with a huge hump on its back with an enlarged head, large upper and lower teeth, and a hooked snout—all within a few weeks of spawning. Pinks live only two years and are very abundant, but are usually looked down upon by Alaskans as trash fish worthy only of being caught by purse seiners for canning. Yet, they're actually a good gamefish on appropriately light tackle.

Pink salmon are small and looked down upon by Alaskans, but still provide good sport on light tackle.

LINGCOD *(Ophiodon elongatus)*

Range: California to Alaska.

Weight: Average 5-20 pounds. The IGFA record is 82 pounds 9 ounces by Robert Hammond in the Gulf of Alaska at Homer in 2007.

By far the largest member of the greenling family *Hexagrammidae*, this fish is neither a ling nor a cod. The long body with dark blotches features a large toothy mouth, and there's no mistaking it for any other fish. Lingcod have become highly prized by anglers, but this excellent-eating fish is no longer abundant. They favor deeper waters, especially in rocky areas and kelp beds, and prefer live baits (including smaller fish being reeled up by anglers) but will also take dead baits and jigs. Their meat has a greenish tinge that disappears in cooking. The much smaller kelp greenling is a common catch in shallow North Pacific waters.

Lingcod are neither ling nor cod, but Pacific anglers prize them for their large size and as good food.

CALIFORNIA SHEEPSHEAD *(Semicossyphus pulcher)*

Range: California south.

Weight: Average 2-5 pounds. The IGFA record is 28 3/8 pounds by Marshall Madruga at Isla Roca Partida, Revillagigedo Islands, Mexico in 1999.

The only important Pacific member of the wrasse family is a most unusual fish. Like the unrelated sea bass, they begin life as females and become males after seven or eight years, when they're about a foot long. Females are pinkish-red, but become black on the head and rear third of the body while adding a hump on the head upon changing sex. The large white-chinned mouth features powerful teeth for feeding on shellfish, though they'll also take fish baits and hit jigs. Most California sheepshead are caught in 20- to 100-foot depths and are excellent eating fish.

California sheepshead are colorful fish found in temperate waters. The author jigged this one in the Galapagos Islands.

CALIFORNIA CORBINA *(Menticirrhus undulatus)*

Range: California to Baja California.

Weight: Average 1/2-1 1/2 pounds. The IGFA record is 7 pounds 15 ounces by Scott Matthews at Mission Bay, California in 2004.

This favorite of California surfcasters is similar to the kingfish of the Atlantic surf and has long been protected from commercial exploitation. Softshell crabs are a favored bait, but worms, mussels, ghost shrimp, and clams also work.

SURFPERCH *(Embiotocidae)*

West coast surfcasters also enjoy catching these fish even though few exceed a foot in length. Most important of the fine-eating surfperch, which readily take the same baits used for corbina, is the barred surfperch *(Amphistichus argenteus)* which has a record of 4 1/8 pounds from Oxnard and is the most common surf species in southern California. The redtail surfperch *(Amphistichus rhodoterus)* grows to 16 inches and is most common farther north from Bodega Bay, California, to Oregon. The rubberlip seaperch *(Rhacochilus toxotes)* frequents sandy bottoms in central and southern

California with three specimens of 1 1/2 pounds taken at Tiburon in 2011 to tie for the IGFA record.

KELP BASS *(Paralabrax clathratus)*
Range: Washington to Magdelana Bay.
Weight: Average 1-2 pounds. The IGFA record is 14 7/16 pounds from Newport Beach, California, in 1993 by Thomas Murphy.

A member of the sea bass family, the kelp (calico) bass is important enough to California anglers that it was put off limits to commercial fishing in 1953. Unlike its Atlantic relatives (such as the grouper), the kelp bass regularly rises to the surface and is usually caught on live anchovies fished around kelp beds.

CABEZON *(Scorpaenichthys marmoratus)*
Range: Sitka, Alaska to California.
Weight: Average 2-5 pounds. The IGFA record is 23 pounds from Juan De Fuca Strait, Washington, in 1990 by Wesley S. Hunter.

The largest of the sculpin family Cottidae is basically an inshore bottom fish and prized as food, though the meat may be bluish-green before cooking. They hit both bait and jigs, and are easily identified by a scaleless body that can range from green to red—and the flaps of skin over the eyes and in the middle of the snout.

OPALEYE *(Girella nigticans)*
Range: California to Cabo San Lucas.
Weight: Average 1-2 pounds. Up to 13 1/2 pounds.

This member of the sea chub family may be the only basically vegetarian fish sought by saltwater anglers. They live along rocky shorelines and in kelp beds, feeding on both plant and animal matter. As a result, moss is often used as bait for this fussy and difficult-to-hook fish that has an oval, compressed body, dark olive-green color, and bright blue eyes.

CHAPTER 4

Understanding the
Marine Environment

In order to be successful, anglers need more than just the proper equipment. Most important, they must understand the waters they're fishing and all the variables that dictate where fish may be and when they'll be feeding. This is no easy read, and for every serious angler it's a lifetime endeavor that will never be completed. Conditions change so rapidly that we're forever trying to keep up, and the only certainty is that those unwilling to change will sooner or later be left behind.

The freshwater fisherman usually deals with a relatively static situation in his favorite pond. The same fish and their offspring are always there, and the relatively few variables such as water levels rarely change greatly. On the other hand, the saltwater inshore fishermen must deal with an ever-changing environment. If all else is the same, there will still be a big difference as the tide and current increase or decrease. Muddy flats at low tide may become productive feeding areas a few hours later, while the slough in the surf providing hot action at low tide could become unproductive as the incoming tide provides more feeding areas for predators.

Fishermen regularly confuse tide and current. Tide is the vertical movement of water—in other words, up and down. Current is the horizontal movement. Thus, it's not a "strong tide," but rather a strong current. Of course, it's those tidal changes that are primarily the reason for currents—and the range between tide levels greatly influences the strength of currents. Tides are the rhythmic rise and fall of sea level. They're rather like the effect you get from tipping a bowl of water back and forth. Tides are basically oriented to the gravitational effect between earth and the moon.

Skipjack tuna are oceanic fish, but when blue water moved right into the beach during August 1999, Kevin Noonan's cast to breaking fish just 200 yards off Sea Bright, New Jersey, produced this 10-pounder on a Hopkins metal.

Since it takes the earth 24 hours and 50 minutes to complete one rotation relative to the moon, high tides will occur 12 hours and 25 minutes apart. Since we operate on the solar 24-hour period, that means the times of high and low tides vary 50 minutes each day. That's why tide tables for any given area can be created years in advance. The height of those tides varies throughout the month, but is also predictable for any given area with the highest and lowest tides (about a 20 percent difference from the norm and referred to as "spring tides") occurring around the full and new moons— while the range will be least two weeks later with a quarter moon and "neap" tides. Further complications result when the moon is closest to earth (lunar perigee), which creates greater tide height variations (especially in conjunction with spring tides) and when the moon is farthest from earth (lunar apogee), which creates lesser variations in tidal height. Finally, there can be extreme tides when the sun and moon are aligned and closest to earth.

Naturally, with more water rushing back and forth in the same time period, there will be stronger currents at the new and full moons. While all of that is predictable, there can be variables introduced by such factors as strong coastal storms that push additional water into bays and rivers, while strong winds off the land in conjunction with a new or full moon can create a "blowout" tide that leaves boats grounded where they would normally be floating at low tide. While most of the Atlantic coast has a semidiurnal tide with two tide changes per day, the Gulf of Mexico is mostly diurnal with only one—and the west coast tends to have mixed tides. The height of the tide varies along coasts and is a predictable factor based on natural formations. Tides range to more than 50 feet in Canada's Bay of Fundy, but are only around two feet in the Gulf of Mexico. Most of the United States Atlantic coast averages five to six feet.

The tide increases on an incoming or flood tide until high tide, and then turns to outgoing or ebb tide until it reaches low tide. Anglers often call high or low tide "slack

Low tides often work in surfcasters' favor as predators such as bluefish can trap prey species in a confined area inside the outer bar.

tide," but in fact that's a function of current that may not coincide precisely with the stage of the tide. Indeed, in some areas it's not even close. The Rhode Island breachways are an extreme case because there's hours of difference between high tide and the beginning of the outgoing current. I realized that when I started fishing at Charlestown Breachway back in the 1960s, but got lucky when I forgot about that gap one bitter cold Halloween night. In those days we didn't have all the sophisticated clothing for cold weather, so after dinner I struggled into three sets of heavy clothes in order to catch the high tide and get a good position at the end of the jetty to cast my plug into the outgoing water, where striped bass often waited for bait to be swept out of the ponds—just as is the case with predators seeking prey at every inlet and river-mouth. I was amazed to find hardly any cars at the lot, and it wasn't until I waddled to the jetty and saw the current roaring in even as rocks were becoming exposed by the falling tide that it dawned upon me I had almost three hours to wait for the proper conditions!

However, since I was there, with rod in hand and already burdened with clothing, I decided to make a few casts from the jetty to behind the surf line anyway. With the northwest wind behind me, my Junior Atom sailed far from the jetty under the brilliant full moon, and I was shocked when the water exploded under it. Within a half-hour I had landed stripers of 38 and 32 pounds with no competition at all, and was able to sleep in instead of fighting the outgoing current mob.

That was a most fortunate occurrence, and certainly not what the angler will normally encounter if he doesn't take tides and currents into consideration when fishing inshore. As a general rule, those factors are critical. Most fishing is poor around slack water, but some fisheries are better then. As a general rule, predators feed when currents present smaller fish to them in orderly fashion rather than having to expend extra energy to track down an elusive baitfish at slack water. The key is to determine just what the species you seek desires in a particular area. For instance, for

Current (note rippled water) is usually necessary even for catching bottomfish such as summer flounder, which these anglers are seeking from shore inside Oregon Inlet, North Carolina.

many years I enjoyed trolling big plugs on wire line at night at Shagwong Reef, only a couple of miles east of Montauk, Long Island. During the fall, I trolled there only on the outgoing tide when the current would bring young-of-the-year weakfish, sea robins, snapper bluefish, blowfish and other fish to the bass as they hung around underwater rocks in 16- to 20-foot depths. My best action occurred during the week leading up to the full moon and the week after, though the few days right around the full moon were tougher. Off the moon, whatever bass bite there was might start slowly but would last through most of the tide before it died as the current slacked. However, on the full moon hits would come during the first hour of the ebb, and then I'd often go three to four hours without a hit before getting another flurry as the current started slacking.

Those stripers wanted a moderate current, but not too much—and the key to catching them was being there at the correct stage of the tide in relation to the moon. That is exactly what local pros learn by experience in their areas. Just as I did there, you can make such determinations by putting in a great deal of time under all circumstances. Or you can watch and listen to what the pros say and do in order to attain the ultimate secret of catching fish—being in the right place at the right time! You'll still have to utilize the proper bait or lure and a technique that works, but until you're able to find feeding fish those other skills are of little use.

Tide stages are particularly important in shore fishing, as some areas may be perfect at a given tide and useless at others. Anglers usually associate high tides with the best opportunities, but quite the opposite is often true as low tides concentrate both bait and fish. Shallow, flat surf is poor on low tides unless the sea is calm enough for surfcasters to wade to the outer bar and cast into deeper water. That can work out well on a dropping tide, but the angler must be alert to the change in tide as water will start filling in behind him and getting back to shore could be dangerous if he hesitates too long. The ideal low tide situation is to have cuts in bars that form sloughs of deeper water with access to the ocean. If there's bait and predators around, that's where they should be, and your effort can be concentrated in the sloughs instead of along the entire beach.

Even well inside bays, there are times when low tide can pay off. I learned that lesson back in the early 1960s with the great wooden plugmaker Stan Gibbs, who took me into Barnstable Harbor on Cape Cod one afternoon. He ran his small boat well up the harbor where the big range of tide had left little but mud flats toward the end of the ebb. Then we got out and walked along the flats to cast his small pencil poppers into the remaining narrow channel that was no more than 50 feet across and usually less. It all looked very peaceful and unproductive, but school striped bass

Wind against current creates rips and breaking waves over high spots where gamefish such as stripers and blues off Montauk Point gather to feed on disoriented prey fish.

exploded on our plugs almost every cast until the tide started flooding and the action stopped as those fish apparently moved out into the bay where they'd be much more difficult to locate.

The key is to take advantage of the tidal situation, whatever it may be. Even though you come to know that a certain tidal or current situation will be ideal, that doesn't mean you can't do even better under other tidal circumstances somewhere else within reach if you just experiment enough and keep your ears open for information.

One of the likeliest places to find predators is in a rip created when current from deeper water hits a shallow area before dropping back into deeper water on the other side. Rips may be formed both in sandy areas (such as Sandy Hook, New Jersey, at the mouth of Delaware Bay, and Nantucket Shoals) or on rough bottoms such as the Montauk rips. These are the most natural feeding grounds of all for predators who can line up at the lip of the high spot and pick off prey swept to them. Once again, current is the key, as there will rarely be any action unless a fairly strong current sets

the feeding process in motion. Once the current starts moving there will often be a surface indication (especially when the wind is against the current) of rippled water or breaking waves—and that will become more intense as the tide drops. By trolling just ahead of the rip, or powering to stay in place ahead of it while dropping jigs back, or by drifting through with jigs, you should be able to attract any predators in the area.

Author unhooking a 50-pound striper which hit a Danny plug trolled at night on a fall ebb tide over underwater rocks at Montauk, where those predators lay in wait for young-of-the-year fish migrating south.

By considering the effect of wind and current, anglers can have good fishing despite what initially may seem to be negative conditions. For instance, a strong northwest breeze combined with an outgoing tide at Montauk Harbor creates a fishable situation since the wind is behind the current. Therefore, it's possible to run a few miles east and duck in under the point or the cliffs along the south shore to fish in good conditions—as long as the return is made before the current swings in—and against the wind. Not only was I able to fish Shagwong Reef with the northwest wind on ebb tide (wind and current together), but the rip formed there also permitted trolling in a stiff east wind on the ebb since the current up against the wind created steep waves at the high spots, which left a smooth area in front of the rip—which is right where I wanted to be! Under those circumstances it was impossible for me to drop back through the rip whenever I hooked a big striper, having to fight it to boatside into the current instead. However, knowing the area and local conditions enabled me to fish effectively.

Offshore currents are more unpredictable than those along the shore. Though there is a rise and fall even out there, you'll probably never notice it, and I doubt that tide per se is of much consequence in the depths. What is important, once again, is current, and that's something which can be affected by many conditions. You may note a strong current from a particular direction in the morning and expect it will change within a few hours, but instead find it running just as hard from the same direction all day. When fishing offshore, look for edges that indicate a meeting of currents or a significant change in water temperature. Sargassum weed and flotsam often gather along those edges, and that makes them extremely attractive to some fish—particularly dolphin and wahoo. Dolphin often gather under even small objects floating in the ocean, but weed lines and large objects such as planks and logs are a sure thing if they're in the area—unless another skipper has been there first! In some cases good bottom structure may be indicated even offshore by rips or upwellings. That's a frequent occurrence as you approach the 100-fathom drop-offs at the edges of canyons, and on humps off the Florida Keys.

Author fights a dolphin hooked along the edge of a sargassum weedline in the Gulf Stream off North Carolina.

Water temperatures were something most of us paid little attention to decades ago. It's a good thing there were lots of fish in those days because otherwise we'd have been out of luck. Water temperature is critical in many instances, and particularly important offshore where there may be few other indications of fish concentrations in vast areas of deep water. The temperature itself can be a good indicator, but even more important are temperature breaks from warmer to colder or vice-versa. Both predators and prey tend to favor those areas, though in some cases the desired species may be located only on

Any object floating in warm waters can serve as an attraction for dolphin. This bull was trolled from the author's boat in the Mud Hole off northern New Jersey from under the dead sea turtle in the background. There were many more there also, but they wised up after this one was hooked.

one side. Many predators exhibit definite temperature preferences. For instance, after many years of checking shark tournament results, biologist Jack Casey determined that June tournaments in the New York Bight would result in many blue sharks but

few of the desired makos if the surface temperature was under 64°F—but that makos would be much more abundant and blues less bothersome over that mark.

These days, no canyon fisherman along the Mid-Atlantic coast goes to sea without checking the latest satellite temperature chart, and that knowledge has lengthened the season when a warm eddy moves into the canyons in June or pockets of water over 60°F persist into December. Yellowfin and albacore tuna are now being caught much later in the year

When surface water temperatures reach 64°F it's prime time for migratory mako sharks, such as this one caught from the author's boat by N.J. Devils defenseman Ken Danyko, offshore of Manasquan Inlet, New Jersey.

Continuing to troll in a Hudson Canyon area where whales were surfacing produced this nearly 200-pound yellowfin tuna. Large yellowfins with extended fins are the same species but are usually called Allisons on the East Coast. Mike Ristori points out that while this one had the extended dorsal, the anal fin was only a stub.

than ever imagined so far north, and even blue marlin are a possibility off New York in May or June if one of those eddies moves within range.

Though we pay attention primarily to surface water temperatures, there's also much to be learned by looking below us. Thermoclines are formed where much cooler water meets the surface layers, and the contrast is often so strong that it shows up on depth recorders as a thin line. Early in the year that colder water may act as a barrier to some fish, so it may be wise to keep baits intended for pelagic sharks above the thermocline. Later in the summer the effect may be quite the opposite as predators seek more comfortable temperatures below the thermocline and baits set deeper tend to produce.

CHAPTER 5

Knots

There are hundreds of knots designed to suit a wide variety of purposes, but anglers are probably best off mastering a few that will serve most of their needs. The quality of the knot can be critical, as an overhand knot in mono will reduce line strength in half. However, there are plenty of knots that are relatively easy to master and which provide 90 percent or more of the line test when properly tied. My personal favorites are the improved clinch knot, Albright knot, blood knot, loop knot, and dropper loop. The Bimini twist, which really isn't a knot, is used to create double lines that are, in turn, frequently utilized for knot tying.

A basic consideration in knot tying is drawing it together properly. Good knots which are tied improperly can pull loose, and anglers must always pull as tightly as the line test will permit in order to ensure there can be no slippage. It's best to tie knots with tension rather than on slack line, though care must be taken that the hook or lure doesn't snap back if your grip is lost. With heavy lines and large hooks, I secure the hook to something on the boat from which it can't slip and pull on the leader with two hands. Modern monos and fluorocarbon leaders are so slick that it's often necessary to tie knots several times and add additional turns in order to prevent slippage— and braided lines are even worse. Indeed, only a few knots work with braided lines. I use the two recommended by Power Pro—the Palomar for terminal rigging, and the uni to uni splice for attaching to backing and leaders.

There's always some loss of strength in a knot, but good ones will provide more than 90 percent when properly tied, with some approaching 100 percent. Friction in the tying process can lower knot strength considerably, so knots should be lubricated before being drawn tight. A little water or spit will do the job nicely. Don't be too precise in cutting off tag lines right to the knot, either. As tight as you may think the knot is, there's always the possibility of slippage, and that little bit of tag end hanging out can make the difference between a knot that tightens further during a fight and one that pulls out. That tag end should always be left at the terminal end, but a neat trim is required in knots that have to be reeled through guides so they won't catch. Line tension helps in tying knots and is critical in some cases.

Unless line visibility is a prime consideration, I normally rig my tackle by creating a double line with a Bimini and then attaching the double to a leader with an Albright knot. The Bimini loses none of the line's strength, and the double tied into the leader with an Albright is much stronger than the line. Since the leader is invariably heavier than the running line, knot strength at the terminal end isn't a big concern as long as it doesn't slip. For instance, if you're using 60-pound leader with 30-pound line, the loss of 10 percent in the terminal knot still leaves you with 54-pound breaking strength in the leader, which remains far greater than the line strength. The only time this becomes a consideration is when the leader is handled with a large fish alongside.

Improved Clinch: This is the basic terminal knot I use for tying hooks and many lures to leaders. It's the basic clinch knot but with the tag end pushed back through the loop created before tightening. In cases where a leader isn't used, I create a double improved clinch knot. That's easy to tie when utilizing a Bimini twist with the double line intact. Once that round end is cut and there are two separate strands, the knot becomes a little more difficult. In those rare cases where a very light line must be used directly, I double the terminal end back over the line about a foot, put

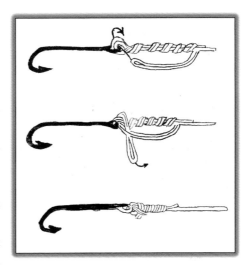

Double Improved Clinch Knot

the loop through the hook eye, and proceed to tie the knot with the short piece of doubled line for improved knot strength and less likelihood of slippage.

Albright: This knot has proven ideal for rigging wire line. I use it both at the connection between the mono backing and at the other end to a 25-foot leader. In that fashion both ends of the line can flow through the guides and fish are reeled right to the boat rather than having to be leadered in. It is necessary to

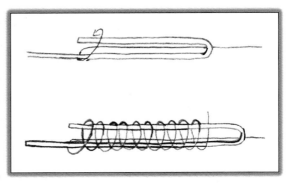

Albright Knot

trim the knots so they don't hang in the guides, but when properly tied the Albright will never come loose. The wire end must be twisted and snapped off right at the knot. Never cut tag ends of wire with pliers as you'll invariably leave a sharp piece that can cut fingers. The Albright requires at least seven turns, and the tag end must be brought through the loop from the opposite direction it went in. Pulling it together evenly is critical, and if any mono loop ends up above the wire it's time to cut and start again. This knot is also my standard for rigging to cast or jig lures which don't spin, as it's perfect for joining two lines of great disparity in strength—such as 60-pound leader to 20-pound line. However, I haven't been happy with the Albright in using braided lines. Even with many added twists I've had heavy mono leaders back out after awhile.

Blood: This knot works well for joining two lines of approximately equal strength. Most of the mono on reels is never used except in big-game fishing situations. Since mono doesn't go bad, anglers can save money and use short lengths of line left on service spools by adding to a depleted spool or stripping back the half of the reel being utilized and tying the new mono in with a blood knot. If tied properly, this is over a 90 percent knot. It is somewhat discomforting to see that knot pulled off the reel by a larger than expected fish, but I've never had one part under such circumstances.

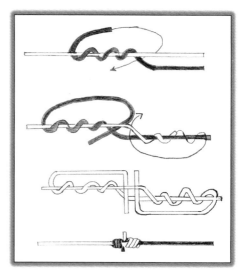

Blood Knot

Homer Rhode Loop: I'm not sure what this knot is really called, but it was shown to me many years ago and has never failed. I always assumed it was too simple to be of high knot strength and worked simply because I used it only in heavy leaders for casting lures that work better on a loop rather than a drawn-down knot. However, a test on a Berkley machine proved it to be well over 90 percent breaking strength. All it involves is forming a loop with several inches of line extending from it. Then pass the end through the lure eye and run the tag end twice through on one side of the loop before crossing over to run it through at least once on the other side before drawing tight.

Dropper Loop: This is a handy knot for making quick rigs in leaders where knot strength isn't a prime consideration.

Bimini Twist: By forming a loop of a desired length, then making at least 20 twists above it, and pulling apart the two pieces while drawing down on the tag end, it's possible to form a 100 percent "non-knot" by securing the twist with a simple overhand knot. Actually, we use overhand knots on both sides plus additional ones around the two lines in order to secure the twist and guard against one backing out. For the long Biminis used in big-game fishing, it's easiest for two people to create the twist with the one at the end moving up the long loop to the twist before pulling the strands apart to create the required pressure. The short doubles used for other purposes can be tied over the knees. Be sure to have tension on the line above you (such as by placing the rod in a rodholder with the reel in gear) and spread your knees to create the pressure. The uncut double is easy to work with in creating an Albright knot. If used with a swivel, it can be looped through the eye, brought back against

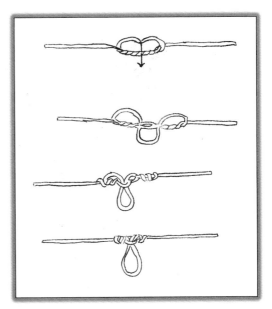

Dropper Loop

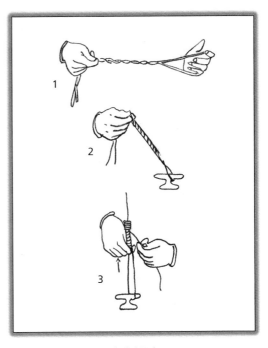

Bimini Twist

itself, and held as the swivel is spun through the two loops several times before tightening by pulling on the swivel. Spider Andresen figured out a way to get around all the line that must be handled in the Bimini, and his Spider Hitch provides a simpler, if not quite as effective, means of creating double lines of any length.

Uni to Uni Splice: Position both the braided and mono lines so they run parallel to each other for 12 to 18 inches. Make a loop in the mono and pass the tag end through the loop and around both lines five or six times before pulling the tag end to secure the knot. Then do the same thing with the braid but put eight to 10 wraps through the loop. Pull the standing lines and watch the two knots jam to form the connection. The mono must be trimmed tight in order to avoid catching in the braid, but one-eighth inch should be left when the braid tag end is

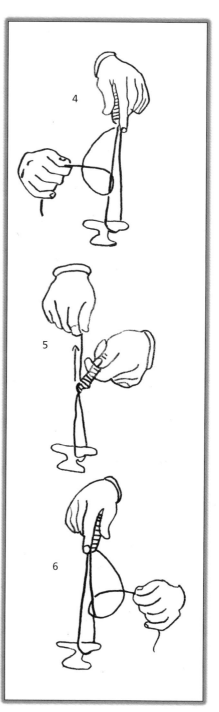

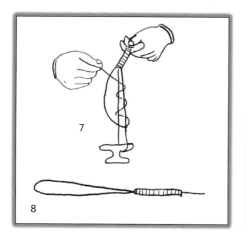

Bimini Twist, continued.

114

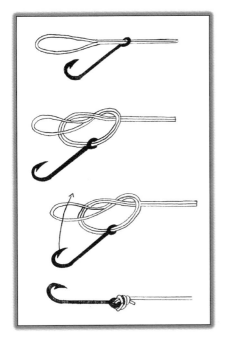

Palomar Knot

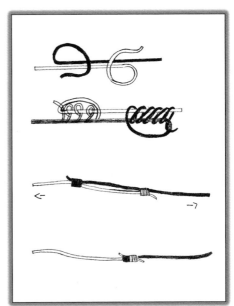

Uni to Uni Splice

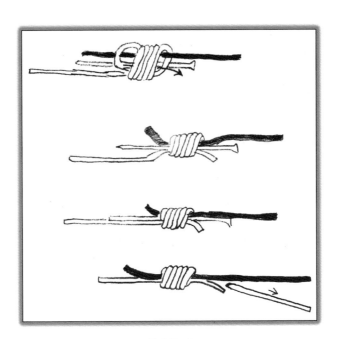

Nail Knot

cut with scissors. It would help to have an extra hand or two when tying this connection, and I advise doing it at home when you're in no rush.

Palomar: This is also a good knot for mono. Make a 10-inch loop in the line and pass it through the hook eye. Do this twice if the eye is big enough. Then tie a simple overhand knot and pass the hook through the loop. Pull on the standing line to tighten, then trim the tag end.

Other commonly used knots include the **nail knot,** which is a standard for connecting both flylines and leadcore to leaders; the simple **surgeon's knot** for quick connection of flyline and leader; the **uni knot;** and **figure eight knot.** In addition, many anglers prefer to snell hooks with turned-up or turned-down eyes. That skill is also handy in creating two hook rigs.

In the case of wire, the **haywire twist** is a must to master. Some anglers simply twist wire around itself and hope for the best. In most cases they get by only because they don't catch big fish. An improperly constructed haywire will slip and break rather easily under heavy pressure, however. To tie, pass several inches of wire through the hook or swivel eye before bending the tag end back and crossing the standard wire to form a small loop. The next part is tricky, as you hold the

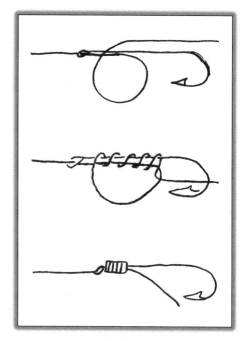

Uni-Knot

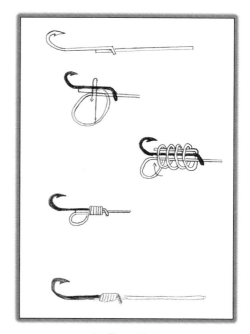

Snelling a Hook

loop firmly between the thumb and forefinger to form a wide V between the two strands—and twist simultaneously to produce a rolling twist with the strands tight to each other rather than separated. If this isn't done correctly for at least three and a half twists, the entire twist will slide up and snap under heavy pressure. The finish is easy, as the tag end is bent so it's at a 90-degree angle to the standing wire and wrapped in several tight coils. Most important is the final step, which involves bending the last inch of the tag end to a right angle and bending away from the standing line to form a "handle" that

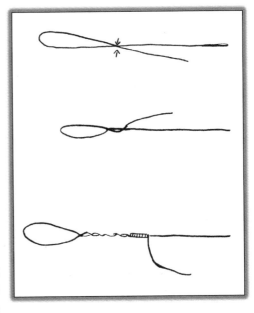

Haywire Twist

is rocked back and forth until it breaks off at the twist. This procedure leaves a smooth end. Using wire cutters on the tag end will leave a burr that can tear a hand.

CHAPTER 6

Rigging

This a broad enough subject to fill several books, but I'll attempt to cover some of the basics in a chapter. When I was a youngster, it was necessary to learn rigging quickly as there wasn't very much pre-rigged gear in tackle shops. That's certainly not the case now, as anglers can buy almost anything all rigged up in a package even at mass merchandisers. However, those rigs usually have more hardware than necessary, and rigs created for the specific circumstances at hand are often more effective.

My general rule is "keep it simple," as almost invariably you'll be better off with a minimum of hardware and knots. Though relatively expensive, fluorocarbon leader material provides an opportunity to use fairly heavy leaders that are practically invisible underwater. However, that fact must be tempered by the stiffness of the material, which can also be a factor in turning fish off under certain circumstances. In delicate fishing, such as drifting baits back to wary tuna in a chum slick, I prefer to do nothing more than attach the smallest hook possible to the end of the fluorocarbon. However, if baits must be drawn back and forth, a build-up in line twist will create an unworkable situation including dangerous looping around the rod tip. A swivel consequently becomes necessary on such leaders. Yet, no matter how small that swivel is, it will create some added weight plus drag on the leader. These are the sorts of considerations that go into creating rigging appropriate to the situation.

A simple fishfinder rig with a fluorocarbon leader and a circle hook through the lower jaw and out an eye socket of this eel makes a good rig for drifting along the bottom for striped bass.

Bottom fishing doesn't usually require such delicate presentations. Still, rigs must be suited both to the species involved and the nature of the bottom. For instance, fishing on rough bottoms is sure to result in hang-ups that can't always be broken out without losing the rig. Therefore, rigging should be very simple. The standard two-hook rig with one leadered hook tied into a dropper loop a leader length above the sinker and another a leader length above the first will work for a variety of fish and is quick to rig. When fishing on wrecks, pros usually eliminate the second hook, as it might get snagged in wreckage when a large fish is hooked. Sometimes the leader isn't necessary, and by attaching hooks directly to dropper loops you'll experience fewer snags. When drifting on rough bottom, any sinker is likely to get hung up, but anglers fishing reefs are able to glide through most of the hangs with egg-sinker rigs. It should be noted that boaters can retrieve most hung rigs rather than breaking off simply by running back over the drift and pulling the rig in the opposite direction.

Rather than tying knots, most big-game fishermen opt for crimping that forms a neat, safe connection. Heavy-duty hand or bench crimpers should be used for best results, and crimp sizes must be matched to the diameter of leader being employed. Crimping should squeeze rather than crush the leader, and it's important to avoid crimping to the edge. Big-game pro Len Bierman proves that point by purposely crimping to the edge on leaders used by his wife Marsha, who has caught hundreds of marlin on light stand-up tackle. The sharply reduced strength of the leader is of no consequence when the marlin is being fought

Ex-heavyweight champ Larry Holmes with a tautog taken on a simple one-hook bottom rig designed to be regularly replaced at minimal cost and time expenditure after getting hung up in rough bottom.

Cut clam on a leadered hook rigged about a leader-length above the sinker is standard for cod taken from wrecks.

119

Marsha Bierman fighting a large bluefin tuna in the winter off North Carolina. Her husband, Len, crimps leaders at the edge so they'll stand up during the fight but can be broken under the pressure of leadering big fish for a quick release.

Heavy mono leaders are needed to stand up to the raspy bills of billfish such as this blue marlin off Venezuela.

on 30-pound line, but when Len is able to grab the long leader for an official release he only has to take a couple of wraps and then jerk in order to snap heavy leader at that crimp edge.

Wire and cable are frequently employed as leader material in big-game rigging, though most anglers now opt for mono or fluorocarbon unless sharks are desired. Indeed, fishermen who started drifting baits deep at night for swordfish during the 1970s soon switched from the traditional wire to mono not only because it wasn't necessary for swords but also to avoid long fights with big sharks instead of the intended quarry. Single-strand wire, often called piano wire, is most popular for sharking. Even makos can't bite through it. Kinking can be a problem, however, especially with sharks that tend to roll up in leaders. Once a kink forms in wire it can snap off in an instant. Anglers must be careful to smooth out any bends in the wire and cut off those that are at severe angles. Multi-strand wire resists kinking but is heavier and can be bitten through by large sharks, as some anglers have found after long battles with huge makos. Many sharkers now use combination leaders with just a few feet of single-strand wire attached to a heavy swivel and then joined to longer length of cable or very heavy mono, which is easier to handle at boatside but won't break should a shark roll up in it.

Though the preparation of leaders is strictly up to the fishermen, those adhering to IGFA sportfishing standards and wishing to be considered should they catch a potential record fish must comply with the rules set up by that organization. The IGFA still doesn't permit the use of wire lines even though they have breaking strengths just as all others. Wire leaders are permitted. Indeed, there is no restriction on leader material. Double lines may be used, though in salt water they may be no more than 15 feet with lines up to 20-pound, but up to 30 feet with heavier lines. Leaders are limited to 15 feet up to 20-pound lines and 30 feet with heavier lines. However, the combined length of the two cannot exceed 20 feet up to 20-pound and 40 feet with heavier tackle.

For live or dead bait fishing, no more than two single hooks may be used no less

Wire leaders are required for sharks, as makos have teeth that can even wear through braided wire, making single-strand wire a must. Mike Ristori with a mako aboard his father's boat.

than a hook's length apart and attached to the bait (not swinging). Treble and double hooks are prohibited. Only two separate hooks may also be used in an artificial lure with a skirt or tailing material. However, gang hooks are permitted on plugs and other artificial lures specially designed for their use.

CHAPTER 7

Techniques

This is another subject that could fill up a book all by itself. It's also necessary to detail it to specific areas and fisheries. Here, I'll review the techniques which I feel are particularly important and of fairly universal importance.

DEEP TROLLING: Surface trolling is relatively basic and easy to learn. However, the volume of fish feeding at the surface is rarely more than a fraction of what may be available lower in the water column. Getting down to those fish while trolling can be accomplished in a number of ways, though all require quite a bit of time, expense, and effort, plus a commitment to master the technique.

The easiest and most direct is trolling with wire line or lead-core. It must be noted that wire line trolling is not legal under IGFA rules, but leadcore is approved.

Wire is far more efficient than leadcore in cutting through the water to achieve depth without weight and is the better bet in strong currents. Leadcore is easier to use but, due to its bulk, works best in shallow waters and where there isn't much current. The general rule with single-strand wire at the relatively slow trolling speeds used for striped bass and bluefish is to let out 100 feet of wire to attain 10 feet of depth. Thus, if you're trolling in 22 feet, 200 feet of wire should put your lure right where you'd normally want it—two feet over bottom where any feeding fish can see it but you won't be hanging up or catching weed. Of course, all this isn't quite as simple as it sounds, since the skipper must be alert to adjust for a variety of conditions. For instance, a larger

Wire line and Luhr Jensen planers are two means of getting down to where fish feed most of the time.

wave, a boat wake, or a sudden increase in current at a rip can momentarily "stop" a boat trolling at slow speed—which is all that's required for the wire to drop to bottom. Getting hung up with wire means you'll have to bring in any other lines that are out and run back uptide ahead of the hang to pull in the opposite direction. Lures will usually pull free in that fashion. If not, run the boat over the spot and maintain headway while pulling on the leader by hand. That's why I use long leaders attached to the wire with an Albright knot so they can be reeled onto the spool.

Wire-line rigs are often trolled from outrodders in order to spread the lines and prevent tangles that can be a disaster with wire. Bunker spoons also work better in that fashion.

Handling wire is a big problem for beginners. Both the more flexible monel and the less costly stainless steel have virtually no stretch and tend to jump off the spool rather than lay on it like other lines. The trick to streaming wire is tension. First, clamp your finger on the spool before taking the reel out of gear. Then strip the leader out past the knot or swivel so nothing will catch in the guides. Wire can now be streamed slowly under thumb pressure, which is reduced as more is out and tension increases. If there are no other lines in the water, all of this can be accomplished in a flash by speeding up the boat. If wire has to be paid out at slow speed, the angler must also stop it with his thumb several times in order to prevent weighted lures from falling to bottom.

How do you know how much wire you have out? Unless you buy a wire marked by the manufacturer (Malin manufactures a color-coded wire line), it's necessary to mark the wire by hand. By far the best bet for beginners is to buy the wire at a tackle shop and have them mark it. In areas where wire is commonly used, marinas with lots of sportfishing docks will have a dock with marks at 100, 150, 200, and 250 feet. Unless you're fishing very shallow waters, there's no need to place a mark before 100 feet. However, should you be regularly working a spot that only requires 75 or 125 feet, make a mark at that spot. Indeed, if that's the only place you'll be using wire line, forget the marking entirely and attach to your backing at that point. If there's no dock marked out for you, the alternative is to lay the line out on your lawn after putting it on the reel and measure the spots to be marked. Remember that the long length of leader doesn't count for depth.

Many materials can be utilized for marking wire. Coated colored wires within phones are very good, but I usually employ vinyl tape, which can be purchased on a card at about $1 for five rolls in different colors. The rolls are too wide, so I pull off some tape and strip them in half before wrapping the pieces on my wire. Be sure there aren't any edges exposed, as these will catch in the guides and slide. Tape rarely lasts more than half a season, but is easy to replace once you get used to it. Any system of marking will work as long as you remember the code. I generally use the same color for a single mark at 100 feet and a double mark at 150 feet. I use another color with a single mark at 200 feet and a double at 250. Using the double marks rather than another color

Wire can be marked to determine depth by wrapping material such as vinyl tape at 50-foot intervals.

is important at night, as then you'll have to feel the marks when setting your line. Though some trollers use only 150 feet and add drails to get deeper, I always employ the entire 100 yards and avoid drails, which sink like a rock if you make a mistake while trolling and require handlining of the leader. In order to get down farther, I slow down or make wide turns. All of this can be avoided with leadcore, which comes with the braid pre-colored with a different color every 10 yards.

Planers may be used in conjunction with mono or braided lines to attain depth without getting involved in wire or adding equipment to the boat. In many cases planers are so efficient that commercial fishermen use them while trolling with handlines. The main drawback from a sporting viewpoint is that long leaders must be used, which require lots of handlining in order to get the fish to boatside. In addition, the heavy tension involved makes it mandatory to place the rod in a holder rather than holding it if you care to do so with wire or lead core. There are many sizes and types of planers, and the angler must find one suited for his form of fishing, as each is limited to reaching certain depths and many can't be trolled at higher speeds without tripping. Rather than rigging them directly onto the line, they can also be rigged

Stan Blum with kingfish trolled with a downrigger off Fort Pierce, Florida.

separately on a heavy line attached to the boat with the line then set in a snap on the planer. Of course, that doubles the work involved as the planer must be brought in after every hit.

Downriggers are very efficient at bringing regular mono or braided lines into the depths, and provide a big advantage in depths greater than those which can be attained by wire line or planers. On the other hand, downriggers also require a substantial investment and lots of effort on the part of the skipper and crew. Basic downriggers consist of a reel filled with cable, clutched cranking handle, boom, and pulley. The lure or bait to be run from any sort of conventional or spinning tackle is run out the desired distance from the ball and then attached to a release clip on the cable. The ball is then lowered to the desired depth, and when a hit occurs the line will pop out of the pin so the angler can fight the fish unimpeded and on tackle as light as he cares to use. Adjusting the tension on the release clip is critical with light tackle so the line will pull free on the strike rather than breaking. Getting that tension correct can be a problem as speed increases in order to avoid having to constantly reset lines that pop free without a strike. Though the amount of cable streamed is displayed on the downrigger, determining just where your lure is requires some guesswork as the forward movement of the boat raises the standard 10-pound ball considerably. The net result is that, depending on speed and current, you may be trolling at only half the depth indicated on the downrigger. This problem can be overcome by experience, but it will take experimentation. You can also try a Z-Wing, which is a combination of planer and weight that can be used to hold lures at greater depths with an outrigger or by itself on a length of rope to

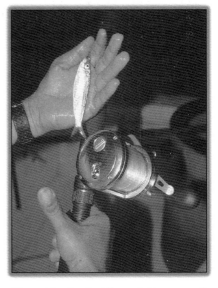

Live sardine hooked through the nose so it can swim and attract predators.

Dead baits must lay out properly in order to look natural and not spin. When a second hook is called for with large baits, the first must still be placed in front with the second less than a length away as not to create a bend, which will cause spinning. These fluke baits are a smelt and squid strip combo and a whole squid (which swims backwards).

facilitate relatively fast trolling. Many skippers at Zihuantenejo, Mexico use Z-Wings and often bail out with a bait trolled about 20 feet below the surface on slow days when billfish aren't showing.

"Doormat" fluke like long fillet baits from other fluke, sea robins, and so on, but the first hook must be at the head with a stinger set so it won't cause the bait to spin.

Downriggers should be retrieved whenever a substantial fish is hooked, as there's a good chance of losing a battle should the mono touch or get tangled in the downrigger cable. If backing down becomes necessary, the cable must also be kept away from the props. Expensive electric downriggers simplify the problem of having to hand crank downriggers every time a fish is hooked or missed, or a pin opens up. However, they also require more complicated boat rigging.

BAITING UP: Placing bait on a hook may seem too simple a matter to be discussed here, but it's probably the most frequent error committed by the casual angler—and I often see the same errors made by those who should know better. The general rule is simple: Secure the bait so it flows out naturally rather than spinning in the water. That applies whether you're drifting, casting, trolling, or even just bottom fishing. Thus, if you're utilizing a baitfish with a single hook or a treble, that bait must be hooked in the head. If the bait has a mouth that opens easily, such as an anchovy, it should be hooked through the jaws. Using a strip bait, the hook must be placed as close to the leading edge as possible while still providing a firm grip—and the end is best trimmed. All of this is intended to prevent the bait from spinning and looking unnatural. Even in bottom fishing, a poorly hooked bait will spin in the current. A

Plug-cut herring are standard among Pacific northwest anglers who mooch for salmon. These baits are rigged to provide a slow, controlled spin.

bait that flows off instead of being bunched is more attractive and leaves more of the hook available to penetrate. Not only do bunched-up baits tend to turn off all but the hungriest of predators, but they result in twisted leaders which further compound your problems. Fortunately, most predators hit at the head of a bait, and no matter how long your bait is they should be hooked with the single hook.

Those toothy fish noted for cutting off baits (especially king mackerel, wahoo, and barracuda) may require a second hook, but the connection at the head is still required. One way to get around adding a second hook is to rig with a long-shank hook inserted far back in the bait while securing the eye inside the head so it will trail out properly.

An exception to the rule about baits not spinning is provided in the Pacific Northwest, where salmon fishermen do exactly the opposite by making their herring baits spin. The plug-cut herring involves cutting the head of a small herring off at an angle and then rigging a two-hook rig around it so it will spin when slowly retrieved or mooched (trolled very slowly). That controlled spin has proven very effective over the years. Another exception involves hooking live baits in areas other than the head for drifting or casting. Inserting the hook in the back or tail creates a different swimming action and often triggers strikes when baits hooked in the head are ignored or just played with. I learned that lesson while giant tuna fishing out of Gloucester, Massachusetts during the 1970s, when a single giant swimming through our slick refused not only our dead baits but also live mackerel and harbor pollock that we had jigged before leaving the harbor. After much frustration, and having tried everything else, I changed the hook in a harbor pollock from the head into the tail area, and that foot-long fish barely got below the surface before the 800-pound giant engulfed him.

Another important point about baiting involves not burying the hook. Very few gamefish see enough hooks to become

Circle hooks are hard to bait, but their efficiency and the lack of harm to fish being released makes them ideal for most bait fishing.

Capt. Ron Hamlin developed techniques for rigging billfish trolling baits that ensure live releases. This is a mullet rigged with the circle hook on top of the head to allow penetration.

"hook wary," as anglers often say. On the other hand, many fish are able to discern unnatural presentations. The weight of the hook plus the leader and any swivel will cause a hooked bait to sink faster and look different. Getting around that problem is often vital to success, but it's rarely the sight of the hook that is the vital factor. However rigged, the hook must either be exposed or unencumbered for the strike. Tuna fishermen can get away with hiding hooks in butterfish by rigging them so the hook is in the soft belly with the point just coming through the thin belly skin so it will pull through immediately. With other baits it may be possible to run the hook just under the skin, but in every case the object should be to present a natural-looking bait with the hook positioned to set immediately in the fish rather than getting caught back in the bait. Not only are hook-ups with ordinary fish missed due to hooks buried in baits, but several times I've seen anglers lose mako sharks after battling them for 20 minutes or more before finding that the hook was caught back inside the bait all the while—and the mako just didn't want to give it up!

The use of circle hooks is becoming more common, as they are more efficient for hooking most fish when using bait, and are far superior in preventing gut-and-gill-hooking, which results in heavy mortality among released fish. The problem with circle hooks is baiting them. Some manufacturers have tried to get around this by angling the circle slightly, but that also results in more swallowed hooks catching in the stomach. The concept involves letting the fish turn away with the bait before coming tight. Captain Ron Hamlin started the use of circle hooks in Guatemala in order to cut down on the mortality of Pacific sailfish, which are all released. Not only was that accomplished, with bleeders now

A quicker means of rigging balao with circle hooks under the jaw, as developed by Mike Murray.

being rare, but the catch rate actually went up. During one three-day trip there I was able to hook and eventually release 24 out of 25 sailfish strikes by simply lowering the rod tip to the fish and reeling tight before lifting (not striking) the rod. It isn't always that efficient, but circle hooks can make you a more successful as well as a more responsible angler in many fisheries. I've already found that to be the case in chunking and clam chumming for striped bass, and while using

Ground chum brings a blue shark to boatside, and is also standard for other sharks, school bluefin tuna, little tunny, bonito, and reef fishing.

both worms and grass shrimp for weakfish. Though the toothy bluefish almost always cuts off hooks tied to mono leaders, I had about a 50 percent success ratio with even them while using bunker chunks intended for stripers. Since the hook pulls toward the jaw, blues have a hard time getting to the leader if they don't cut it off on the initial hit.

CHUMMING AND CHUNKING: Chumming may well be the most effective and universal technique for catching a wide variety of species ranging from bottom-fish to tunas. Billfish are among the few that don't seem particularly attracted to chum, but even they are caught occasionally in slicks. Chunking is a form of chumming in that chunks of bait are used rather than ground chum, and the two methods are frequently combined.

Just about anything can be used for chum, but oily fish make the best ground chum. Nothing can beat the menhaden for that, as they are the most abundant and oiliest fish along the Atlantic coast and in the Gulf of Mexico, where millions of pounds are taken each year by purse seiners for reduction into fish oils and meal. Menhaden (also known as mossbunker, bunker, porgy, and fatback) are also netted in vast quantities for bait and chum. Party boats in the Metropolitan New York/New Jersey area have heavy-duty meat grinders aboard with which to create their own fresh chum. Most anglers are able to buy frozen ground chum (generally in five-gallon buckets or smaller cans) or even in dried form. Where menhaden aren't available, mackerel, bluefish, herring, and other oily species will do. Most Florida anglers obtain chum in the form of frozen logs, which are created from a variety of ground-up fish and scraps. Chum logs can also be created from other baits more suitable for various species. For instance, winter flounder aren't fish eaters, so chum is formed from ground clams to which corn kernels and/or rice are often added for additional attraction.

Ground chum can be used in either fresh or frozen form. Fresh chum is ladled over the side either full strength or mixed with water to make the supply last longer. Frozen chum is hung in the water by some means (the simplest is to overturn the can into a mesh bag and tie it overboard) and slowly dissipates. In either case, the idea is to create a slick on the water and a scent trail that will lure fish to your boat. That slick will usually be obvious, especially on a rough day, but can't be seen when frozen chum is dropped to bottom in a chum pot to attract bottom feeders such as flounder. Chumming with ground bait is probably the most common means of fishing for sharks, and the primary weapon for party boats in the New York/New Jersey Bight area seeking bluefish.

Chunking is very similar except the chum is presented in the form of chunks of baitfish rather than ground bait. Menhaden, herring, mackerel, butterfish, and many other small, abundant, and inexpensive fish are used in that fashion for species that don't rely on scent very much. It's generally best to cut chunks smaller than those used for bait, but also to adjust according to the size of fish. For instance, bluefin tuna anglers seeking schoolies use small chunks of butterfish while those trying for giants prefer large chunks of menhaden, which are not only more attractive but also discourage the schoolies. Whereas even very large sharks will swim around in slicks looking for something to eat, tunas generally zip right through a slick and will only stick around if chunks are being swept back to them. Key West guides are able to chunk such glamour species as tarpon, permit, and cobia as well as snappers by obtaining shrimp boat "trash," the by-catch of shrimp trawling, and dribbling small cut or whole fish and shellfish astern. For tarpon, use trash consisting mostly of small

fish, while for permit try to find "crabby" trash. Another unusual but very effective chunking material is the waste product of clam processing plants—the bellies. Striped bass, especially schoolies, would rather eat the bellies in any case, and that bait is especially effective when squeezed to release the juices when being used as chum on top—as well as when used in a chum pot.

The basic method of chunking involves throwing a good quantity when first

Menhaden are chunked for striped bass, bluefish, red drum, and other bottom feeding gamefish.

arriving at a fishing spot, and then settling down to a slow, but steady dribble so as to attract without filling the quarry. This can be done at anchor or on the drift, depending on the situation. Chunks may also be mixed with ground chum, especially if there's no worry about attracting sharks or bluefish, and a chum pot is often dropped to bottom with chunks when chunking in relatively shallow waters for stripers with bottom rigs. Whereas a strong current is an aid in spreading a chum slick, it can be a problem for chunking as the chunks move away too quickly or don't sink to bottom near the boat when you're seeking bottom species. In such areas it's best to get started at the beginning of a

Butterfish serve as both bait and chunking material for tunas and bluefish.

tide and "salt" the area astern with chunks. Cut back on chunking as the current increases and throw them forward so as not to be chunking for any boats anchored downtide of you. A means of getting chunks where you want them involves placing them in a weighted paper bag and lowering it to the bottom on a line before a snap of the line breaks the wet bag and deposits the chunks where they'll do some good.

Once fish come into a chum slick or chunk line they'll frequently stay there and refuse to spread to others even yards away. Therefore, it's important to be the first on a spot. Alternately, you can try the same area late in the day or at night when there may be little or no competition. Fresh chunks with slime intact are always better than frozen ones, though there's rarely any big difference when fish are really turned on. Indeed, I've had some of my hottest striped bass chunking while using solidly frozen

menhaden chunks, which actually act like individual chum pots as they thaw.

Chumming can also be done with live baits, and that's the norm on the west coast

Author fought this giant tuna on Stellwagen Bank off Gloucester, Massachusetts, while Larry Cronin ran the Boston Whaler and wired the fish before the author placed the straight gaff.

Wiring an 800-pound class tiger shark from the Reelistic offshore of Indian River, Delaware.

Capt. Bob Montgomery leaders a cobia over a wreck in the Gulf of Mexico out of Key West as another follows.

where live anchovies and sardines can be bought in quantity. Live baits are flipped around the boat and will usually stay there in order to seek protection from tunas, wahoo, barracuda, yellowtails, and other large gamefish. Some fishermen pinch baits in order to have them swim erratically and create more attraction. Chunks can be used in combination with live baits as long-range skippers out of San Diego discovered when they tried the time-honored east coast chunking technique and found that large yellowfin tuna often preferred chunks to live bait.

That's hardly surprising since tunas are conditioned to feed on just about anything dead falling through trawler nets or being thrown over by draggers and shrimp boats.

The use of tiny live grass shrimp as chum for weakfish goes back many decades in bays along the Mid-Atlantic coast. They are dribbled astern a few at a time and lines can be baited with several of the shrimp or with other baits such as seaworms. Once established, grass shrimp chum lines usually produce so many weakfish that tiny lures such as shad darts and small bucktail jigs are just as effective. Stripers and tautog are among other species attracted by grass shrimp chumming.

The one constant involved in chumming is the need for water movement. There normally must be some flow, though in areas of strong currents fishing is often best at the beginning or end of the tide when the current isn't too swift. Slack water is occasionally productive when the fish have been turned on before the current slacked. Movement is particularly critical in sharking, as those fish are spread over large

132

Author leaders a black marlin off Panama before release. Billfish often spit out their stomach during a fight, but swallow them back.

Leader men must be alert with fish that may jump at boatside, as this tarpon is doing to Capt. Robert Trosset at Key West.

areas rather than concentrated on a particular piece of bottom or dropoff. When there's no movement the chum falls straight down and anglers have to hope that a shark will be swimming their way. On the other hand, with good wind and current the slick will spread over miles and bring curious sharks within range of baits near the boat.

THE END GAME—GAFFING, NETTING, AND TAGGING: While fighting fish is the most important aspect of the sport, the fish of a lifetime could be lost if the angler isn't prepared for the end game. There are a few general rules to keep in mind while preparing to boat a fish. Most important is getting a good shot the first time. All too often there's panic at the wrong moment as gaffs or nets are being swung wildly and to no good effect—frequently resulting in the loss of the fish. There's rarely any reason to make a desperation stab. Anglers who overpower large fish and then attempt to boat a "green" fish are asking for trouble and frequently get it. Mako sharks are particularly dangerous and have wiped out many a cockpit while sending anglers scrambling for safety. Fish should be fought to the point where they can be led alongside for an attempt at boating that leaves little to chance. Wherever possible get the angler forward of the gaffer. If leader must be handled in order to bring the fish within reach, the leader man should be in between. Either the angler or leader man should literally present the fish, broadside if possible, to the gaffer so he has a clear shot at the head or shoulders. Do this as smoothly as possible in order not to panic the fish. A key factor in not losing fish at boatside is keeping their head in the water. It often takes only a little shake on some slack to dislodge a hook from the hole it's worn during a fight.

In big-game fishing the boat is usually kept in gear at very slow speed in order to maintain tension and plane large fish along the surface. Anglers on drifting or anchored boats must be alert to any movement by the fish and be prepared to dip the rod tip in order to clear props and rudders. In open boats it's best to work larger fish off the bow where a sudden move

Gaffing a giant tuna at Prince Edward Island. The wire man should bring the fish within reach of the gaffer so he can get a good shot in the head.

under the boat will rub the line only over bottom paint instead of line-cutting metal. Try to bring the fish alongside upcurrent or uptide so there will be less chance of it diving under the boat. Wherever possible, move with the fish so as not to end up with an angle forward or aft and a consequent lack of control.

One of the most common mistakes by small-game anglers is reeling a fish almost to the tip of the rod. That leaves the fish far from the person trying to boat it, and can lead to rod breakage. Bring the fish only to about a rod length and then lift the rod to slide it toward the mate. Try to avoid gaffing fish farther back than the shoulder, as you won't have as much control and will be ruining meat. Especially avoid gaffing toward the tail, as large fish are extremely difficult to control in that fashion. The gaff should be placed over the fish and brought back in one motion, which will also swing smaller fish into the boat in a single sweep. In the case of large fish which are notoriously wild when gaffed (especially dolphin and cobia), there must be a clear area behind the gaffer to an uncovered fish box so the fish can be deposited and the top replaced in an instant while everyone available sits on the cover to make sure it doesn't get knocked off.

Billing a black marlin in Panama.

Special care must be taken with billfish and sharks, which can do a lot of damage as they surge forward or jump. The head should be slightly forward of the gaffer when it's hit and pinned quickly against the boat if possible. I prefer to hit sharks in the gills, as gaffs often bounce off their tough skins. Small billfish and all those to be released are billed (be sure to use gloves to avoid tearing your hands up) rather than gaffed. This is another tricky proposition since everyone must be alert to a last second jump that could drive that bill through flesh. Never get directly in front of a bill when preparing to grab it, but rather slide it slightly past you and reach down to grab sideways with both hands. Though long leaders permit the capture of large fish long before they can be fought close to the boat, they represent a great danger both to the person leadering and anyone else who may get caught in the slack leader should the fish take off again. Wherever possible, I prefer using short, or wind-on, leaders and having the fish reeled to the boat where leader handling is either not necessary or only requires a pull in order to present the fish for gaffing.

Netting of striped bass is becoming more popular now that 90 percent are released by anglers. Lou Truppi will find that can be a problem with treble-hook plugs.

Standard straight gaffs with shafts four to eight feet are used in most cases, but in big-game fishing it's often best to utilize flying gaffs-in which the head detaches under pressure when the fish is struck. The detached head is secured by a heavy line to a cleat and, hopefully, any jumping that the fish might do will be 20 feet away instead of in the boat. A maximum of 30 feet of gaff rope is permitted by IGFA rules, which also limit the overall length of gaffs and nets to eight feet and prohibit the use of harpoons. Flying gaffs are used primarily for large billfish and especially for sharks, which tend to roll when hit and will tear a straight gaff out your hands if they do so. Tuna, even giants, only move forward and don't jump, so they can be handled with a heavy straight gaff.

Gaffs heads come in a variety of gaps, varying from two to 16 inches, between shaft and point. While large gaps are best for big fish, it's very difficult to gaff smaller fish (especially those with roundish bodies such as wahoo) with such gaffs. Much smaller sizes are far more effective with such fish, and gaffs can even be fashioned out of large fish hooks with the barbs filed or bent down and then wrapped on a fiberglass

Mike Ristori demonstrates there's no problem netting big stripers such as this one caught by Pete O'Connor on a bunker chunk at Shrewbury Rocks, New Jersey.

shaft. There are also smaller hand gaffs with very short shafts that are used in small boat situations for lip gaffing large fish and pinning them to the side of the boat while a hook or lure is removed prior to release. Those gaffs may also be carried by surfcasters to aid in beaching fish. Bridge and pier fishermen seeking large fish utilize a bridge gaff that consists of a very large treble attached to heavy cord that's lowered to a fought-out fish laying on top by running it through a shower curtain clip over the fishing line. A quick snatch once the bridge gaff is alongside the fish allows the fisherman to handline the catch up to his platform rather than taking a chance on breaking off by trying to lift with the fishing line. Naturally, bridge gaffs should never be used on fish that are to be released.

The most important point to remember in netting fish is only netting from the head. Trying to push a net through the water at the tail of a fish is a recipe for disaster as the fish will sense the net and dart away—frequently breaking taut lines or pulling hooks.

Even more so than with gaffs, it's vital that the angler bring his fish to the netter on the surface for a very measured lifting with a slightly forward motion. Wild stabs or digging underwater with nets almost never works. Nets come in many sizes, and the angler should obtain one or more suited to his style of fishing. Small nets are easiest to use when boating small fish, while the largest hoop sizes are best for salmon, halibut, large fluke, and striped bass. Avoid using nets for sharp-toothed fish as they not only ruin nets but might even cut through before you get them aboard. Also don't use nets when fish are hooked on plugs bristling with treble hooks. You may well end up with a treble in the net while the fish hangs outside the mesh ready to shake off—and then you'll still have to spend more time trying to get those hooks out of the mesh than before resuming fishing. Few anglers use rubber nets, but they do eliminate problems with toothy fish such as bluefish.

The best bet in a release situation from small boats is using a long enough length of heavy mono or fluorocarbon leader so most fish can be lifted aboard without worrying about gaffs or nets. Even when keeping fish, that method avoids most of the mess as there are no gaff holes to create bleeding. Smaller fish can be swung aboard with heavy enough tackle, but once again the angler must not reel almost to the tip as that will result in a fish hanging in the air and, quite possibly, a broken rod. Reel the fish to within a rod length and lift your rod to swing the fish toward your waist in one smooth motion.

Many fish can be handled from small boats by simply grasping them with a lip lock, just as freshwater bass fishermen do with their favorite quarry. I use that method with striped bass that are too large to swing aboard. Their jaws result in rough fingers, but rarely any cuts. Fish with teeth or those so heavy that they require more than a lip lock can be handled with a gill-cover grip when subdued at boatside. Be sure you place your hand under the gill cover and not into the gill rakers,

Jay Cassell's blue marlin is lifted alongside Hawaiian Tropic off Key West for removal of hook. This position is dangerous, as the marlin could push forward and do damage with its bill.

which will shred your skin and also possibly kill a fish intended for release. Fish with narrow and rigid tail sections can be grasped from that end. That works well with tunas if you can get at the tail; because the tuna lacks an air bladder and therefore has to keep swimming in order to live, grabbing the tail section can be a challenge. Jacks are easy to handle by the tail, but it's best to wear gloves to avoid being cut by their scutes.

Tagging adds excitement to release fishing. In the case of smaller fish, they can be handled on deck as a tag is inserted by hand. Putting a cloth over their eyes tends to calm them down just as is the case with birds that get hooked. Tagging sticks are used on large fish that must be left in the water. AFTCO makes a nice commercial stick, or anglers can create their own with a broomstick and a hose clamp to hold the pin provided by National Marine Fisheries Service tagging programs. Most tagging is done by scientists, but volunteer anglers are the prime source of tagging in several programs. Jack Casey started tagging sharks during the 1960s at the old U.S. Fish and Wildlife Service Lab at Sandy Hook, New Jersey, but after the creation of the National Marine Fisheries Service that program was shifted to Rhode Island. Sportsmen not

Fish without significant teeth can be lifted aboard with a lip-lock, as demonstrated by Al Malanga.

Capt. Harlan Franklin lifts a permit from the flats at the Marquesas out of Key West by grabbing the tail.

only do most of the shark tagging, but even support the newsletter sent out to participants. Those who are active in sharking can obtain free tagging kits from NMFS Cooperative Shark Tagging Program, NOAA/NMFS Lab, 28 Tarzwell Dr., Narragansett, RI 02882. Billfish and tuna anglers are urged to get involved with the Cooperative Game Fish Tagging

With its bill pointed away, this hook can be removed from the marlin, but if it doesn't come out easily, the fish will be better off if the hook is clipped for a quick release.

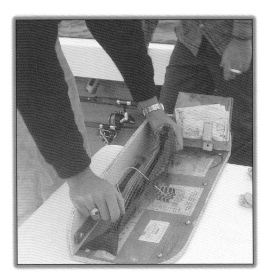

Capt. Al Anderson of Point Judith, Rhode Island, has the tagging of school stripers with American Littoral Society tags down to a science.

Program, NOAA/NMFS Lab, 75 Virginia Beach Dr., Miami, FL 33149 in the Atlantic—and the same program at NOAA/NMFS Southwest Fisheries Center, P.O. Box 271, La Jolla, CA 92038. Anglers joining the American Littoral Society enjoy the unique opportunity to tag any saltwater fish of their choice by buying ALS tagging kits. Those tags are applied by hand with a needle. Contact American Littoral Society Fish Tagging Program, Sandy Hook Highlands, NJ 07732, phone 732-291-0055.

CHAPTER 8

Boats & Electronics

O nce again we have a book-length subject to be squeezed into a chapter, thus allowing only some general advice. First, and most important, is whether you should own a boat. Manufacturers won't want to hear this advice, but the fact of the matter is that many people who own boats never should have gotten involved in what's become a very expensive hobby. Before considering a purchase, consider several factors. First, take the capital expenditure for boat and power on one side of the ledger. Then add the basic cost of insurance, dockage, winterization, electronics and

other boating gear, plus an allowance for the inevitable repairs and the variable costs (depending on usage) of fuel and bait, to the capital outlay. Next figure how many days the boat will actually be used. For most working people that may amount to one or two weekend days per week, if the weather cooperates, plus vacation time if you don't travel somewhere else. Given the relatively short boating season in most parts of the United States and Canada, the average boater may end up using his boat 20 or 30 times in a year. The value of your time spent in working on the boat and cleaning it after each trip isn't even calculated. Now put the interest that could be earned in a safe investment with that capital expenditure on the other side of the ledger along with all the yearly expenditures

Starcraft aluminum 16-footers on trailers were fine in the 1960s for fishing Cape Cod waters, as the author did with Jimmy Andrews and from his own when catches of big bass in protected waters were routine.

and divide by the number of days fished. What you'll find in most cases is that you could have chartered a boat to fish the same number of days while having a professional guide you to fish you may not be able to catch on your own—after which those fish will be filleted and you can climb in your car to drive home while the crew cleans the boat!

All that being said, many anglers still want to own boats no matter how impractical they may be. Though I finally started chartering in 1984, it was the same for me from my first 16-foot Lyman lapstrake wooden boat in 1954 to the $100 20-foot pirogue carved out of a log by Trinidad craftsmen and powered by a 12-hp West Bend outboard with which I fished the Caribbean from 1960 to 62—not to mention the 16-foot Starcraft aluminum boat that served me well in Pleasant Bay, Massachusetts, during the mid-1960s until I trailered it to Horseshoe Shoals off Hyannis and watched rivets pop loose as the boat crashed off steep waves while I bailed with one hand and held my bluefish trolling rod in the other. It wasn't until 1969 that I started running modern Mako center consoles, which ranged from 19 to 25 feet, over the course of 19 years before switching to a 28-foot center console Aquasport with a nine-and-a-half-foot beam in 1988. In a center console, that extra beam makes all the difference over the standard eight-foot-or-less trailerable beams, especially when chartering, as anglers can walk all around the boat with ease. After doing without protection for decades and hardly ever going out without foul weather gear on or handy, I also highly recommend curtains on center consoles. They can be rolled up to allow maximum fishing room, but when running, curtains also provide protection from spray, wind and cold.

Though I've put in a great deal of time fishing from big boats, and occasionally running them, I'm basically a small boat guy. I like being in control of everything from the center console and mixing with friends and customers rather than sitting alone on a flying bridge while a mate does everything I normally handle on deck while seeking fish at the same time. Best of all, I don't need a mate if one of my children isn't available, and can still jump aboard at any time, cast off the lines, and fish the boat by myself. That's an important consideration for the recreational boater, as putting together a crew can be a problem in itself—and getting that crew to share expenses is another matter altogether.

You're the only person capable of deciding just what boat is suitable for your purposes. The first consideration has to be finances, and I strongly recommend not going into debt in order to get started. It's bad enough being forced to deal with all the expenses involved with a boat without having to pay off a note besides. There must be no worse feeling than watching a beloved boat being repossessed. Boats rank with the worst investments, as they not only steadily decrease in value but do so at a very fast rate. On the other side of the coin, this leaves very good buys in used boats sold by those who found they really didn't have the time to fish as much as they thought they would. Modern fiberglass hulls should last for decades, but be sure to get expert opinions about power plants. If in doubt, buy something smaller and less expensive than what you're looking for. You can always trade up after getting your feet wet, but won't be as vulnerable if things don't work out. Seaworthiness is always the most important factor with a boat intended to be used outside inlets, but focus on just what type of fishing you want to do most of the time and buy a boat with that in mind rather than worrying about the one or two offshore trips you'd also like to make. Do those with friends or charter a boat and you'll be way ahead. Another common mistake involves men buying boats with the family in mind. Inevitably they end up with something more expensive than required and not as good for their main purpose. Worst of all, they may find that their better half still doesn't want to move very far away from the dock—if at all. Do you really need that cabin, or those cushioned seats in the bow—or even a head? Far better to spend less money for a "toy" to your liking and let those in the family who want to put up with any inconveniences come aboard while the others do things they enjoy.

Power plants are a source of constant controversy, and all have their good and bad points. Inboard engines are generally more economical, but may not provide the speed desired and are usually hard to work on. Diesel engines are great for economy, durability, and safety, but they cost much more than gas inboards and only pay off for those who use their boats steadily. Outboard motors are the best bets for most small boaters as they provide speed and easy access. Fuel consumption is a problem, but the modern breed of outboard is greatly improved in that respect. The Mercury Opti-Max technology provided me with better mileage and greater reliability before their Verado four-strokes improved outboards in both respects. All the major manufacturers produce very efficient four-strokes now. While they are somewhat heavier, the quiet operation is a far cry from the outboards I grew up with. To be sure, they do cost a bit more, but the economy combined with quiet operation, hardly any smoking, and quick starting make the difference well worthwhile. Combine that with longer warranties and the outboard becomes a best bet as, if worse comes to worse, it can be lifted off the boat and replaced within hours.

Electronics have come a long way since I started staring at Lowrance's "little green box" in 1969 as that original flasher provided a bottom mark (as long as it wasn't too deep) and blips above the bottom might be interpreted as fish or bait. That was actually a very good unit once I got used to it, and I'd like to be able to make the catches of big stripers today with much more sophisticated electronics that I made in those days. Of course, at that point I was in seventh heaven just having that information after years in that pirogue in Trinidad. It didn't even have a compass! By comparison, what we have today on small boats would have been considered state-of-the-art in ships a few decades ago. Fishfinders are now very sophisticated, whether inexpensive LCG (liquid crystal graph) units or fancy color scopes. Once again this is an area where the boater must consider just what he'll be doing. For instance, that inexpensive LCG may be perfect inshore, but it won't reach bottom in the canyon and may not pinpoint a deepwater wreck. However, if you'll never be going that far offshore, there's no need for such capabilities.

What every boat needs in addition to a fishfinder is a VHF radio and a GPS (global positioning system). Like the fishfinder, these units have become relatively inexpensive. The VHF is both your lifeline and a source of fishing information, while the GPS will locate you precisely on fishing spots as well as help get you home. No electronics substitute for a compass, and it's important to remember that while GPS will provide a straight line to your destination, it will do so over rocks, land, and other boats. Your boating skill must still be combined with electronics in order to survive at sea. Radar is a great addition, especially in areas where fog is a regular problem, but it's rather bulky and costly for most small boaters.

Author's first fiberglass boat, when he was director of field testing for Garcia, was this Mako 19. With only a compass and a Lowrance flasher, it still produced lots of stripers from Long Island to Cape Cod.

CHAPTER 9

Shore Fishing

There's a world of shore fishing opportunities in salt water, which is fortunate for those subject to seasickness. Some anglers do so well from shore they rarely, if ever, get on a boat. However, most of us mix both pleasures. It isn't even necessary to go offshore in order to catch big fish. One of the largest gamefish of all, a 1,784-pound tiger shark, was taken from a pier at Cherry Grove, South Carolina, in 1964 by Walter Maxwell. Sharkers have also done well from shore at Cape Hatteras and from both coasts of Florida. Even glamour fish such as sailfish, red drum, cobia, king mackerel, and permit fall to pier fishermen who have devised all sorts of special techniques to deal with their environment.

Surfcasting is a universal sport in salt waters, though there's little similarity between casting big plugs and live eels into rocks for stripers at Montauk, throwing large baits and heavy sinkers with 12-foot rods for red drum at Hatteras, and casting a small jig on one-handed tackle for small game along a calm Gulf beach. Yet, in each case there's something special about catching a fish from the beach that could be more efficiently sought from boats. I prefer sand beaches and usually figure that anything caught while casting a lure along a long stretch of surf is something of a miracle to really be appreciated.

Surfcasters wading to the outer bar around low tide are catching blues at dusk but must be careful to get back as tide rises and fills in the slough behind them.

That being said, the surf can be very productive at times. Indeed, there are occasions when predators have prey pressed so tightly to the beach that boaters must edge in as close as they can get and virtually cast lures on the beach in order to catch anything. Those days make up for the many when all the action is just out of reach over the outer bar. Catching fish in the surf isn't all that challenging when there's a blitz going on. Just "match the hatch" as best you can, especially in terms of size and shape. If that's a problem you can cast a small treble hook with a weight ahead of it to snag a live bait and leave it there for a fish to pick up. Popping plugs that don't resemble the bait at all are also often effective in blitz situations, as the noise and splash gets even stuffed predators turned on enough to slash at something which they have no room to swallow. Quite often you're better off casting to the fringes and especially just behind the school of bait being attacked. At times the fish actually under the bait won't look at anything else, and on other occasions predators with teeth will cut you off after hooking up there. There's less likelihood of such difficulties on the fringes, and it's often possible to raise unseen predators for several minutes after the school has passed—and they probably won't be fussy like the ones right under the school.

It's those more normal days and nights when fish are scattered and there's no competition factor to create mistakes that separate the pros from other surfcasters.

The best time to learn your beach is at low tide. Any sloughs will stand out, as will deeper bars. Concentrate on the sloughs, but also check out those bars as the tide builds. Gamefish like to feed in active water where the prey can't see them as well. Therefore, waves creating white water where there's enough depth for predators to

Diving birds and breaks signal a bluefish blitz along the Jersey Shore.

swim is a likely place to cast surface and very shallow-swimming plugs. Concentrate on working the edges of bars where they fall into deeper water on both sides of a slough. Note every little tap and see if you can detect a pattern that will provide an indication of how fish are feeding that particular day. For instance, though both sides look the same to you, fish may be feeding only on the north side of a slough this particular day, and until you recognize that pattern, you'll waste too much time in the wrong places.

As a general rule, the best time to fish the surf is a day or two after a storm as predators tend to be most active when the waters are still somewhat rough and roiled. After the surf settles with a wind off the beach, the waters often get so clear that your quarry can read the name

Aftermath of a bluefish blitz! As the fish move south, they leave behind thousands of peanut bunkers (baby menhaden), which beached themselves on waves to avoid the slaughter.

on the plug. Especially at night, you may be able to see fish swimming around and still not get a hit from them. One of the best times to be on a heavily fished beach is at daylight after a big offshore storm the day before. It may be too soon for good fishing, but a bonanza in broken-off plugs at the high tide line may await the sharp-eyed!

One trick that works for a variety of fish is the use of a teaser ahead of the main lure. The second lure really isn't a teaser at all, but a small and fairly weightless lure with a hook in it that is rigged on a short, stiff piece of leader from a swivel eye or dropper loop. Flies are ideal for this purpose, as are small plastics such as three- and four-inch Felmlee eels. Whether fish respond to the smaller lure or get excited at the sight of a larger bait fish (your plug, metal or jig) chasing that fly is anyone's guess, but there are times when most of your fish will be taken on the teaser—and not necessarily just the smaller ones. Another trick surfcasters employ to throw small lures works the opposite way. A popping plug with the hooks removed has a length of leader attached to the rear eye with a fly, tiny spoon, or jig at the end. The popper attracts attention to the small lure, which is just right for such often wary species as the little tunny (false albacore, "bonito") and Spanish mackerel.

Tackle for surfcasting can vary greatly, depending on conditions, and doesn't necessarily have to be heavy. Seven- to eight-foot spinning rods with fairly stiff actions are suitable for a wide variety of areas with light surf or on good days everywhere except in rocks where fish must be horsed in. Those rods should have long butts to facilitate long two-handed casting. The longest rod I use is a nine-and-one-half-foot one-piece Seeker that covers rough days and casting big pencil poppers and metal, but is still light enough to handle for hours of casting.

Author with a 15-pound bluefish so stuffed with bait there was no room for more. It still hit a metal lure tipped with a peanut bunker!

Baitfishing in the surf may not be as exciting as casting lures, but it can be very effective and is generally a lot less work. Though lighter rods can be used for most purposes, the 10- to 12-footers come in handy on rough days when big sinkers are required to hold bottom—and are standard in North Carolina for big red drum due to the large baits used. A variety of rigs will work under varying conditions, though one of the most common is the fishfinder, which allows fish to move off with a bait as the line passes through a plastic sleeve attached to the clip of a pyramid sinker that's designed to dig into sand and hold. After being cast out, most anglers put their rods in sand spikes and wait for bites. Fish often hook themselves as they come tight, though there are times when fishermen holding their rods will do much better. A very important point is to set a relatively light drag on rods placed in sand spikes, which themselves must be pushed into the sand as far as possible. There are few things more heartbreaking than watching a favorite rod and reel being dragged into the wash by the "fish of a lifetime." Ironically, when those rods are retrieved by others casting across the area, the "monster" often turns out to be of quite modest size. Prime baits vary with areas, but cut oily fish (such as menhaden, mackerel, and mullet) is hard to beat. The heads of such baits are not only good, but often better than body slices for the largest fish. Clams are usually the top producer of striped bass in the Mid-Atlantic surf, particularly after a storm has tossed many surf clams up on the beach. Florida pompano specialists use clams along the northeast surf, but those south of there swear by sand fleas.

Landing fish in the surf presents somewhat different problems than in a boat. The undertow, especially in a rough surf, often defies all efforts to get a big fish on the sand. Surfcasters usually don't have gaffs, and certainly not the long ones employed by jetty fishermen, so they count on being able to work with the waves in order to get big fish ashore. Most beaches have a sharp drop, and even if it's not very deep the combination of it and the undertow may prevent the angler from moving his fish. Standing up on the beach and cranking won't help as you'll have to wade in as far as possible and try to grab the leader when a wave provides some lift.

Steve Goione helps land a school striped bass plugged on light tackle at Normandy Beach, New Jersey by veteran surf angler and tackle shop owner Ernie Wuesthoff.

Rep. Jim Saxton (R-NJ), former chairman of the House Fisheries Conservation Subcommittee, discovered that teasers such as this Red Gill sand eel imitation are deadly when cast from boats as well as the beach.

CHAPTER 10
Conservation

Conservation has always been a concern for sportfishermen, but today it's far more than that as state and federal governments have become involved in preserving the fisheries we've been blessed with and improving those that have been overfished. While most anglers are in favor of that intervention, few really understand the complexities that have become part and parcel of fisheries management. Just a few decades ago I used to spend a few days saltwater fishing in Florida where and how I pleased, and the only personal decisions to make involved whether I'd keep anything caught. Now I must first buy a license if I'll be fishing on my own (rather than on a charter or party boat or from a fishing pier that will have purchased a blanket license to cover their customers), and I'll have to study several pages of conservation regulations applying to almost every saltwater species of consequence in the state to determine open seasons, minimum and, in some cases, maximum sizes, bag limits, and so on—well as what species are off limits altogether. That contrasts with just a few paragraphs to summarize all the freshwater regulations.

Huge mothership operations from the Soviet Union and other eastern bloc countries devastated many American fisheries in the 1960s and 1970s before the 200-mile limit was established in 1976. This trawler was transferring to a Soviet mothership in the Mud Hole—not much farther from New York Harbor than the 12-mile limit in effect in 1975.

The same thing is happening all over with saltwater licensing long a reality on the West and Gulf coasts, and moving rapidly up the Atlantic coast toward the areas of greatest resistance from New Jersey to Massachusetts. Whether or not there are licenses, anglers are faced with a plethora of regulations. In addition to those adopted by the states, there are regional and federal rules to be considered. The states long ago organized into regional fishery management associations on the Atlantic, in the Gulf, and on the Pacific. For many years these associations were little more than debating societies with no real powers except by almost impossible-to-achieve unanimous consent, followed by uncertain implementation by the individual states. It was the migratory striped bass crisis of the early 1980s that brought about federal backing for regional management plans to overcome the traditional states rights attitude that fish within state waters at any given time were only that state's concern, even if they may have been spawned elsewhere or put on poundage while in other jurisdictions. As a result, the Atlantic States Marine Fisheries Commission (ASMFC) Striped Bass Management Plan had the teeth in it to require cooperation by every state within the migratory range. The success of that plan led to similar plans for just about every other inshore species of importance to sport and commercial fishermen that is primarily caught in state waters.

A congressional reorganization plan over three decades ago changed fishery management at the federal level. The old Bureau of Commercial Fisheries in the Department of Commerce used taxpayer funds to encourage exploitation of "underutilized" species such as the Atlantic bluefin tuna, which resulted in massive depletion. Saltwater sportfisheries at the time were included in the Interior Department's Fish and Wildlife Bureau, but the reorganization plan combined the two agencies into the National

Though it was PCBs dumped into the Hudson River by General Electric, rather than conservation concerns, which forced New York to stop commercial fishing for striped bass in the Hudson River in 1976, that species has made a great comeback in the second most important migratory spawning river. Pros like Tony Arcabascio now catch lots of bass like this near the Statue of Liberty.

151

Bluefish used to be automatically kept in vast numbers by anglers who really had no use for a species that is delicious fresh but doesn't freeze well. Now more than 50 percent are released. Bobby Correll holds a blue trolled by his wife, Mary Agnes.

Marine Fisheries Service (NMFS), which is part of the National Oceanic and Atmospheric Administration (NOAA) within Commerce. Since then, NMFS has controlled fisheries in federal waters while working with the regional commissions on those species that live in both federal and state waters.

During the 1960s and early 1970s, American waters offshore of the 12-mile fisheries jurisdiction in effect at that time were plundered by huge mothership operations, mostly from the Soviet Union and other Iron Curtain countries, and one species after another was greatly diminished. Cod, haddock, pollock, mackerel, herring, red hake, silver hake, and many other species were affected by those fisheries. I joined with other recreational fishermen to form an organization called the Emergency Committee to Save America's Marine Resources in 1972, and was its executive director as we got a 200-mile fisheries limit bill introduced into Congress by Rep. Norman Lent (R-NY). That bill soon had many co-sponsors as the concept of protecting our fisheries—such as many smaller countries were already doing—overcame opposition from the departments of State and Defense as well as politically-powerful California tuna seiners. The Magnuson Act was signed by President Ford in 1976 and gave the U.S. a 200-mile fisheries jurisdiction while also setting up a system of regional fishery management councils. Those councils are made up of people involved in fisheries who are nominated by governors and appointed by the Secretary of Commerce. They work in conjunction with NMFS and the regional commissions to regulate fisheries, though NMFS has exclusive rights to the pelagic species which, in the cases of tunas and billfish, also fall under the purview of the International Commission for the Conservation of Atlantic Tunas ICCAT).

All of the domestic organizations hold public hearings on proposed fishery management plans, which are then publicized in outdoors columns and often attract attention even from the general news media in coastal areas. The public is encouraged to attend those meetings and to comment either there or by writing. If the fishing public really did get involved, many of our conservation problems would soon be resolved. During the fight for the 200-mile limit we were able to get a great many fishermen to write their congressman and senators seeking their support for putting an end to the foreign invasion of our waters. The volume of letters received was so great that even the objections of powerful government agencies and lobbyists were overcome in just four years. Imagine what could be accomplished if that energy could be harnessed on a regular basis!

Voluntary conservation on the part of anglers has become a vital factor in preserving and improving coastal fisheries. In some cases, such as striped bass, sportsmen are literally recycling 90 percent of what they catch, which is in sharp contrast to the old days. Imagine what modern migratory striper fishing would be like if, like the days of abundance during the 1960s and 1970s, every fish over 16 inches long was

The use of a Boga Grip allows anglers to pick up fish for weighing and photos before a quick release. This was at Chesapeake Bay Bridge Tunnel.

going into the box. Especially in cases such as this, where millions of recreational anglers are involved, the new conservation ethic is vital to preserving a healthy fishery as even minimal daily limits of one or two bass a day soon involves removing millions of fish from the population. The right of the public to harvest reasonable numbers of a public resource should be inviolate, but each angler should retain only what he's sure to use rather than automatically boxing everything, as was the case when I grew up and spent much of my time trying to give away surplus catch. Now I feel a lot better about what I release to fight another day while still retaining whatever will go on the plate that night or very shortly thereafter instead of taking up space in the freezer. Sportsmen can hardly pressure netters to modify their often wasteful practices unless we do our part to ensure the viability of fisheries for the future.

CHAPTER 11

The Rules of the Game

Just as in any other sport, there are rules of our game though the very nature of the pastime makes those "rules" among the most loosely observed of all sports. The International Game Fish Association (IGFA) is the official arbiter of the sport, and those of us who are serious about it try to observe those rules as closely as possible even in everyday fishing. The IGFA is run not only by president Rob Kramer and the trustees, including such public figures as Guy Harvey, Joan Salvato Wulff, and Bill Shedd of AFTCO, but also member clubs all over the world. Consensus is required to change rules, and some have indeed been changed over the years—such as longer double lines that have made it possible to catch giant tuna on lighter gear and the legalizing of plugs with treble hooks. Yet, many common angling methods that are considered sporting in various areas (such as double hooks rigged to West coast lures, trebles for East coast live baits, and the use of wire line) remain prohibited for record purposes. That's not to say that catches made in such fashion aren't recognized as sporting on the local or state levels—or even by most other fishermen. Fishing is the most universal of sports and it's whatever one may want to make of it as long as state and federal regulations are observed.

Many of the IGFA rules are lightly observed for other than record purposes. Anyone merely touching the rod, reel, or line (short of the leader) of an angler fighting a fish disqualifies that fish under the rules, but it would still be considered a legitimate catch by other

The IGFA Hall of Fame in Dania Beach, Florida is a must visit for anglers.

anglers unless real aid was provided. That the angler hooks and fights the fish all the way to boatside or beach by himself is the essence of catching a fish. Fish can be credited to boat crews no matter how many people handle the rod, but no angler can legitimately claim to have won a battle with any fish unless he or she has fought it from start to finish without aid. I've always encouraged my charter customers to continue the fight even when they're hurting or afraid of losing the fish. In most cases, that's no big deal. However, there are occasions when we are all tested with a fish too big or too strong for the tackle or circumstances. As with anything else in life, we can accept the challenge and respond to it or give up when the going gets tough and pass off the rod. One of these days I'll probably get in over my head, but I've fought fish as long as 12 1/2 hours (a big swordfish on 30-pound off Salinas, Ecuador, that was lost when something underwater hit the line at night) and never thought of giving up. If it ever comes to that, I'll still not pass the rod over but break the line because the fish will have won the one-on-one sporting battle and deserves its freedom rather than capture by a mob. That's my sporting ethic, but in this universal sport it's not one that everyone must follow. Fishing is, first and foremost, for enjoyment, and those not seeking recognition can make their own rules to suit their standards and conscience. Hopefully, most will opt to respect the resource as much as those of us who have been in the game for decades.

Membership in the IGFA is a good investment, especially since it includes the annual World Record Game Fishes, which lists all records (including the new Junior Angler categories) and includes all the rules as well as articles and other useful information. The IGFA has a beautiful new headquarters and Hall of Fame just off Rt. 95, within a few miles of Fort Lauderdale. Every angler traveling to that area should set aside a few hours in order to visit it. Contact the IGFA at 300 Gulf Stream Way, Dania Beach, FL 33004; phone 954/927-2628 or e-mail IGFAHQ@aol.com.

CHAPTER 12

Enjoying the Sport

Fishing can be as competitive as we care to make it, or totally non-competitive. Many anglers live for the thrill of big-game tournaments or king mackerel contests that often involve big money. Others like to get involved in smaller area contests for species such as striped bass, bluefish, weakfish, and fluke, which may involve smaller amounts of money or just prizes. Then there are many others who want none of that pressure in what they regard as basically a contemplative sport. Yet, just about all could agree there is nothing wrong with competing against yourself. Indeed, that has been an unending lifetime excitement for me as I've maintained records of every

Tournaments aren't for everyone, but the Dinardi family enjoys all the festivities associated with them—and don't mind the pay-off they've received in the Mid-Atlantic $500,000, when everything went right on their Absolut-ly.

Once you've fought enough, there may still be fun to be had by taking the hooks off a popper and teasing charged-up fish such as these amberjack over a wreck off Carolina Beach, North Carolina, into hitting right next to the boat and making a run before they spit out the plug.

day of saltwater fishing since the first in 1945 and summarize the results yearly so I can tell exactly how many fish of which species have been caught over the course of 55 years. Many anglers have only a vague idea of how many fish they've caught during an active day, but I got used to committing all that to memory as a youngster and still have no problem doing so. Carrying accurate hand scales permits weighing of most fish to be released, and others can be measured. A pretty accurate weight can be derived for billfish and tunas by using the following formula—length times girth squared, divided by 800.

Most important are the records of largest fish of each species that I'm constantly trying to better. That gets tougher with each year as standards improve and there are fewer "new" species to be added to the list. In cases of important species where I'm unlikely to ever best my own mark (such as my 61-pound striped bass), there can be additional classifications such as largest from shore, or by casting, or from particular states or areas. The possibilities are as endless as your interest, and that's something that will never fade once you've been bitten by the livelong fascination of saltwater fishing!